HIDDEN TREASURES

EDINBURGH VOL II

Edited by Claire Tupholme

First published in Great Britain in 2002 by
YOUNG WRITERS
Remus House,
Coltsfoot Drive,
Peterborough, PE2 9JX
Telephone (01733) 890066

HB ISBN 0 75433 962 9
SB ISBN 0 75433 963 7

FOREWORD

This year, the Young Writers' Hidden Treasures competition proudly presents a showcase of the best poetic talent from over 72,000 up-and-coming writers nationwide.

Young Writers was established in 1991 and we are still successful, even in today's technologically-led world, in promoting and encouraging the reading and writing of poetry.

The thought, effort, imagination and hard work put into each poem impressed us all, and once again, the task of selecting poems was a difficult one, but nevertheless, an enjoyable experience.

We hope you are as pleased as we are with the final selection and that you and your family continue to be entertained with *Hidden Treasures Edinburgh Vol II* for many years to come.

CONTENTS

Stephanie Rodden	20
Miriam Sakram	21
Greg Summers	21
Yannick Onifade	22
Cheryl Lonsdale	23
Hayley Edwards	24
Gary Whiting	25
David Ritchie	25
Michael Ranken	26
Allan Walker	26
Jade Mason	27
Natalie MacKinnon	27
Steven Cameron	28
Siobhan Doig	29
Abeer Rehan	29
Michael Addy	30
Danielle Christina Inglis	30
Stephanie Cant	31
Ashley Carse	31
Ewen Lowrie	32
Martin McConnell	32
Gregg Cameron	33
Jamie Gilchrist	34
Melissa Pitkeathly	35
Ewan Murdoch	35
Graham Sless	36
Nicolle Carswell	36
Leigh DeRighetti	37
Nick Anderson	38
Dionne Scott	38
Jade Rutherford	39
Carol Moir	40
Emma Patrizio	40
Alanna Swan	41
Kris Whiting	42
Danielle Maher	42
Jade Knox	43
Natasha Todd	44

James Hall	88
Lisa Liddle	88
Becky Crook	89
Jessica Williams	89
Megan Hughes	90
Joanne Baker	90
Alex Honhold	91
Laura Morrison	91
Laura Wilson	92
Sarah Maxwell	92
Josie Morris	93
Ben McClellan	93
Tony Stuart	94
Josh McQueen	94
Leigh Kasperek	95
Fraser Henderson	95
Dianne McKenna	95
Jack Kennedy	96
Tom Watson	96
James Mackintosh	97
Amar Singh	97

The Mary Erskine & Stewart's Melville Junior School

Imogen Adderley	97
Adam Hamoudi	98
Simon Osborne	98
Shona Scott	99
Sebastian Mylchreest	99
Annie Armstrong	100
Ewan Mitchell	100
Hilary Taylor	101
Michael Clark	101
Ruairidh Morrison	102
Joe McGregor	102
Lauren Mercer	103
Euan Williamson	103
Riona MacGillivray	104
Lewis Harding	104

The Poems

HIDDEN TREASURE

'What's so good about them?'
The teacher enquired.

The boy replied (rather dreamily):
'My hidden treasures are at the top of the highest mountain,
The bottom of the deepest sea,
Flying miles above the Earth with the stars and the sky!
They may not be in my schoolwork,
They may not be in sport,
But I assure you, they do exist,
In the dream I dream every day!'

Douglas Thomson (12)
Cargilfield School

HIDDEN TREASURE

I am your hidden treasure!

With me you will fear nothing,
You will be brave in everything you do,
You will not hesitate in trying new things,
You will push yourself to the limit.

Without me you will be timid and not enjoy life to the full,
You will fail in competitions and under pressure,
Without me little good will happen to you . . .

I am confidence!

Gemma Sole (11)
Cargilfield School

HIDDEN TREASURE

My hidden treasures is not what it seems,
My hidden treasure sparkles and gleams.
My hidden treasure is not silver or gold,
My hidden treasure will never, ever mould.
My hidden treasure is not something you eat,
My hidden treasure does not dissolve in the heat.
My hidden treasure comes from a beach,
My hidden treasure is in the shape of a peach.
My hidden treasure is the colour pink,
My hidden treasure will not fit in a sink.
My hidden treasure is as pretty as a flower,
My hidden treasure has nothing like power.
My hidden treasure lies in the sand like stone,
My hidden treasure cannot scream, talk or moan.
My hidden treasure is up in my room,
My hidden treasure is hid behind a broom.
My hidden treasure is nothing like a dog,
My hidden treasure just lies there like a log.
My hidden treasure is deep in the pool,
My hidden treasure, I think is really cool.
My hidden treasure I would never, ever sell,
My hidden treasure is a shell!

Alex Wilson (11)
Cargilfield School

HIDDEN TREASURE

My hidden treasure stows away,
At the bottom of my garden.
My hidden treasure sleeps by day and comes out by night!
My hidden treasure snuffles its wet nose at its youngsters.
My hidden treasure hibernates in the midst of winter
And creeps out into the delight of summer.

My hidden treasure grazes on unusual things,
My hidden treasure only comes out on my call
And has many hidden talents.
My hidden treasure is very shy, spiky and surprising,
My hidden treasure will scare any dog,
So I'm really proud that my hidden treasure is a hedgehog!

Charlotte Nisbet (10)
Cargilfield School

HIDDEN TREASURE

My treasures are inexpensive but special,
They join me at night and offer me the gift of peace,
With all their comfort they give me a place,
Where my thoughts can wander
And I can easily travel far in that world.

At dusk I wait,
Curious about the surprises that lie ahead.

For every night these treasures are different
And I can only imagine what might enrich me this time.

As I am snugly curled up in my bed,
Waiting . . .
For sleep to throw his blanket over me
And lead me to my dreams, my treasures!

Tineke Dusse (11)
Cargilfield School

A BOY OF 10

What does poetry mean to a ten-year-old boy?
Stories with a meaning,
A meaning of what?
Words strung together,
In verse or maybe not.
Or is it a load of tot?
A meaning to me would be,
Now let me see,
I have it,
The life of my granddad,
Who deserves some verse,
He made it fun to read,
I will always thank him for that,
Because to read is my future
And I know to gain knowledge
Will be my reward.
When I learn why we have poets who write life in verse,
To make us realise how much we have grown
And make us laugh at our own tone,
As we see the humour in the lines
And see the light of the seeds that were sown.
Then we can sit back and look forward to our
Grandchildren who we will pass on our life
And hope they will remember us as well as I have
Because when I was seven, I learned to be sad,
My granddad passed on,
I learned that the people we love can't be around forever
And now I am 10, the sadness isn't so bad,
He will be in my heart forever,
For this I am glad.

Daniel Martin (10)
Comiston Primary School

4

DOWN IN THE DARK, DARK CAVES

The dark caves in England
Were thought to have gold in them
Which sparkled like the shining sun
On a hot summer's day

A boy from England heard about the gold
And he thought he could make a fortune out of it
If he got his dirty hands on the shining gold

So the next day he gets kitted up like
An astronaut going into space
And his parents didn't know
What he was about to do

He asked a friend to go with him
But he was not sure about it
Like a lost animal not knowing which direction to go
Then his friend said, 'Okay'

They set off after they had their lunch
They got there in mid-afternoon
They went in and it was very dark
Luckily they had torches
They didn't reach the gold yet
They were very excited
They laughed and screamed
And they made a piece of rock fall
Like an atom bomb being dropped
But they laughed and another piece of rock dropped
And they started to run
And the whole place started to fall to pieces
They managed to get to the entrance
It took them 3 years to make it again.

Shaun Rogerson (10)
Comiston Primary School

WHEN MARTIANS ATTACK

Up in space, upon Mars,
There are things you may not like,
Martians, monsters, scary things,
Boy it'd give you quite a fright.

So if you're not careful,
It could be the plate for you,
With a big monster's knife and fork,
You might look quite a fool.

Anyway Mars is a long way off you know
And no one yet has touched Mars,
So I think it is quite safe.

When or if you go to Mars,
Don't get scared now,
You might see holes or burrows,
Nothing to be scared of.

In fact they're probably hiding from *you*,
You scary person, you might become friends,
Sounds quite cool, friends with a Martian,
A pen pal of course.

Iain Mortimer (10)
Comiston Primary School

SEEING STARS

There may be stars in the skies,
But there are stars in the eyes
Of children, who perform on a stage.

They may sing or may dance,
Act out a story perchance,
Every night learning scripts by the page.

Lots of fun it may seem,
To follow life's dream,
But really they've worked very hard.

It's a challenge, an ambition,
To reach the position
Of gaining an Equity Card.

Joanna Aithie (10)
Comiston Primary School

SPRING

The grass begins to grow this time of year
There is no snow
The trees start to bud
Say goodbye to mud
The flowers in the garden begin to grow
Daffodils, crocuses and snowdrops
Are then on show

The lambs come out to play
The darkness falls away
Squirrels come out their winter sleep
In search of nuts they buried deep
Mad March hares dancing on the hills
To watch them play is such a thrill

Mum brushes away cobwebs
Spiders are made homeless
There's a fresh spring look
Our house is now spotless.

Stuart Shand (10)
Comiston Primary School

THE WEATHER

The weather can be horrifying
Or it can be quiet and cloudy,
With birds soaring and gliding
And even sunny with a slight breeze.

Stormy weather destroys civilisation and nature alike causing chaos,
Horrible hurricanes and terrifying tornadoes sending debris flying,
With thunder and lightning striking trees and churches,
Rain bucketing down, soaking absolutely everything

Clouds - cumulus, stratus and cirrus formations,
Floating lazily by like a dream,
A bird gliding by gracefully,
In this beautiful, wonderful stream.

The sun, shining bright,
A gentle breeze blowing past,
The only thing disturbing it being children laughing,
Some might argue this isn't proper weather,
But if it is, it's probably my favourite.

Stuart Watson (10)
Comiston Primary School

SEASONS

Winter begins and ends the year,
Cold as ice and wet as tear,
Snow and ice, wind and rain,
Every year it is the same.

It's not so cold now, it's spring,
If you go outside you'll hear the birds sing,
Lambs are born once again,
A nice plant blooms now and then.

It's summer now and it is nice,
Warmer days and longer nights,
Every child is out of school,
Busy in the swimming pool.

Now it's autumn and it is warm,
Harvest time, wheat and corn,
Leaves on trees will not be green,
It gets dark at Hallowe'en.

Harry Brickell (10)
Comiston Primary School

MY CAT, SMOKEY

In the dark, I can see
Two bright circles coming towards me,
They bound past,
Then come back to me,
But it was only my cat, Smokey
With a mouse in her mouth.
I love it when she is happy,
Rubbing her soft cuddly fur against me.
Purring gently, allowing me to tickle her tummy,
But when she is angry,
I need to watch out,
Her tail flicks fast,
Ready to bite my finger and toes.
I like her best, when she is sleepy and relaxed,
She lets me stroke and cuddle her gently,
Making me feel happy inside.

Jennifer Dodds (10)
Comiston Primary School

THE SNOWY WINTER

One snowy winter you could
Hear the wind whistling and whirling.
The children playing with the snow
Just outside your front garden,
Hearing the snow falling off the roof
And hitting the ground.
When you walk through the park
Listening to the snow
Crunching when you walk on it
And feeling the snow hitting your back
And people shouting everywhere.
When you're asleep you can hear wolves howling
Up in the hills and hear Santa in his sleigh
Coming on your roof and falling down the chimney.
On Christmas Day the children are all excited
And when they get their new sledges they go and play on them.

Michael Newlands (9)
Comiston Primary School

THE ROSE

The rose is a red, red flower
As red as strawberries, fresh and ripe
As red as our blood running through our veins
Like water through a pipe
As red as the peppers and tomatoes
Waiting to be put in a sauce for spaghetti
As red as a heart-shaped piece of confetti
As red as the poppies from the First World War
As red as red wine ready to pour
As red as cherries on the cherry tree
As red as anything red I can see.

Jussie Eastwood (9)
Comiston Primary School

SONG POEM

You can get many types of songs
Classic, rap, love and rock
Different people like different types
That they like to dance to at night
Abba has classic
Misteeq has rock
Elvis has love
And NSync has pop
Hip hop and pop
Are my favourite two
'Cause they have songs that sound so new
Every one has different taste
That means no songs to go waste
All music bands have an idol
And all songs have to have a title.

Hazel Cummings (10)
Comiston Primary School

SPRING

Spring, spring, such a wonderful time
As buds peep through the ground
And the snow begins to disappear

Crocuses, snowdrops and daffodils too
Hyacinths in shades of pink and blue
That you can watch for a day or two

My next-door neighbour all dressed in yellow
And the sun reflects on my friend's cello

The lambs are born in a youthful field
As spring's kindness is revealed.

Euan Moffat (10)
Comiston Primary School

WINTER

I feel glad when it is winter,
A new season has come,
The soft and freezing snow,
The whistling of the wind,
Ice will come
And birds will tweet.
People walking down the street,
Rubbing their hands together,
Snowmen have been built
In the gardens of the young.
Snow is soft on your hands,
But as cold as a freezer.
Children playing snowball fights
In their gardens.
The trees are swaying
In the wind,
Winter is here,
Until next year.

Lauren Goldie (10)
Comiston Primary School

LEAVES IN A SQUALL

The leaves stumble and trip
In a buffeting wind,
Spinning and weaving,
Pitching and rolling in a whirlwind sky.

Suddenly the wind changes,
Violently, neighbouring leaves
Get tossed into a puddle,
Sodden, wet and glued to the ground.

Others glide and drift
In their own skydive formation,
Rolling around without a care,
Then disappearing into the clouds forever.

William Elsom (10)
Comiston Primary School

MY ONE DAY OFF SCHOOL

I've just finished my holidays
And I'm feeling cool,
But the only thing I'm sad about
Is I have to go back to school.

I've been sledging all through the holiday
And I've been having loads of fun
And now I'm thinking forward,
I have to do thousands or more boring sums!

In the future I'll be doing some
Real easy-peasy pictures
And I'll be falling half-asleep all day,
When I'm listening to boring lectures.

Oh, here we go again,
I'm off to school,
What's that I hear?
School's off, golly gosh,
That's cool!

Ewan Muir (10)
Comiston Primary School

THE CITY

The city is busy, messy
With people running about the place
Like ants in a hurry
The cars in a queue
Down the main street
The shop's getting full of people
The sweets getting taken by the high school
Into the bus stop where they wait for a bus
Evening lights bright and colourful
People in the pub, getting drunk
With beer and wine
Cars were down Princes Street
The police fight to hold the protestors
Back to the street
The train's stopping to have a break.

Builders dig up gravel from the street
They build bridges and make new roads
Buses scream as the brakes work hard
To stop from hitting other cars
Factories with men and women stand back
To watch a teacher make a volcano
And watch it erupt
The bell rings to let the children go out
The sun goes down and the city goes quiet
The lights go off
Darkness comes again until morning.

Nathan Hunter (10)
Comiston Primary School

A BATTLE FROM THE AGES

As the sun rises, the battle begins,
The side that defeats all surely wins.
With swords gleaming in the sunlight,
It will be sure to be a great fight.
In the distance a horn blows,
The half-moon still up, armour glows.
Bowmen aim up, shoot past their ears,
The enemy's screams, the other side hears.
Opponents retaliate charging with fury,
Slicing, stabbing and slashing wildly.
General's eye-to-eye, watching each other like hawks,
Flaming arrows flying in the air as if it were Guy Fawkes.
An assassin hiding in a gorse bush,
His general smiling, he gave a big blush.
Pulling back on his bow,
He couldn't wait to let go.
One more second and they would win,
He let it go and realised he had done a sin.
The assassin had killed his own leader,
He then knew he had to be a good pleader.
For he had lost his side their freedom,
For a long time they really needed some.
He then took his sword from its cover,
Stabbed himself and shouted, 'Mother!'

Ross Irvine (10)
Comiston Primary School

MY FAVOURITE THINGS

My favourite things are soft and nice,
One's called Sugar and one's called Spice,
He's so big and she's so small
And they are really the best of all.

I cuddle them each night and day
And after school we sit and play,
We have a party and make a din,
Oh no, now my mum's come in

To tell me tea will be ready soon,
So I had better sort my room,
Then I'll go and watch TV,
With Sugar and Spice upon my knee.

You see they are my teddy bears,
They wait for me as I climb the stairs,
To go to bed because it's late,
So goodnight to all, from Kate.

Kate O'Malley (10)
Comiston Primary School

PIGS CAN FLY

Percy is a pig extraordinaire
He comes from a planet, I know not where
He flew into my life out of nowhere
A pink blob looking for adventure!

So that same day my new friend and I
Flew into the sky
Soaring over the River Thames
And winking to the London Eye.

People say it's nonsense
People say it's an exaggeration
People say it can't be true
But it is . . .
Pigs *can* fly!

Ross Chinnery (10)
Comiston Primary School

SEPTEMBER SCARE

Before September 11th, the world was happy
It was a windy day, but sunny
Then all of a sudden, the sky became dark
Everything came to a halt and froze
The war between America and Afghanistan was about to start
Was the world coming to a close?

I remember coming out of school
Couldn't wait to kick my ball
I didn't really understand, why the towers had to fall
Still I wait and wonder, if things will turn out right
I thought there was only one God, so why do people continue to fight?

I remember the day the towers came down
I hope it helps us see
A peaceful loving world is how it should be.

Murray Douglas (10)
Comiston Primary School

CANDY WORLD

Candy World is good,
Candy World is great,
Last year I went there with my mate

There are candystick trees
With chocolate bees
And sugar grass
That grows when you pass.

The moss is candyfloss
And the coffee is made of toffee.
You play polo with Rolos
And the stars are Milky Bars.

Karen Cossar (10)
Comiston Primary School

CATS IN THE CAT SHELTER

Thin cats, fat cats, fit cats, lazy cats,
They are all different.
Big cats, small cats, cheeky cats, funny cats,
All wanting you to take them home.
Cuddly cats, nervous cats, sweet cats, scared cats,
They all have their own personality.
Siamese, Persian, tortoiseshell, blue tabby,
There are many different types of cat.
All of them cuddly and bright,
But sometimes they might get into a fight!

Catherine Lourie (10)
Comiston Primary School

RUGBY

Sunday, Sunday,
This is the time with my pals.
This is the day,
I have some fun running
Like a bullet train.
You can see Murrayfield lighting up,
I'm dashing like a puma,
I can't wait until,
The game starts.
I've got the ball,
I'm sprinting in and out,
I'm dodging,
Dummy passing . . .
Try!

Stuart Steel (10)
Comiston Primary School

TAO, THE CAT

Tao has chocolate-coloured paws
And sapphire eyes that glow.
He can open latches or doorknobs, big or small.
He lies in front of the fire contentedly,
Washing methodically behind his ears.
Tao has a black face, it looks like a mask.
He has monkey-like hind legs
And he has a tongue like a dog, but smaller.
He has a smooth coat and silky in a way.
That is Tao.

Philip Anderson (11)
Davidson's Mains Primary School

A WHITE SIGHT

Almond eyes begin to focus on me,
Peering out of the old, leafy tree.
Ears flickering about the silent air,
Clashing on its snow-white hair.
Its white tail, frantically wags about,
Its wide, thick tongue licks its snout.

This downright ugly dog is a breed not fit for travelling,
But a creature who awaits the affectionate care
From a human calling.
It lies down on the grass, trying to pass some time
And remembers the beautiful days of his prime.
This honourable dog is gifted with an amazing life,
Living through trouble, hardship and strife.

William Kwok (11)
Davidson's Mains Primary School

THE LYNX ATTACK

I see an evil shadow crouched low in the darkness,
I see a fearless face, a wild cat staring into my eyes.
I hear my heart beat faster, faster in fear
As I jump up into a thin, shaky tree.
I hear a lynx silently slinking along,
Ready to strike me away.
I smell fear emanating from my small thin body,
I feel frightened as I jump off the tree to my feet,
I don't dare turn to fight the lynx.
I think my life is about to end but I decide to run,
I think I'm lucky this time, but what will happen next?

Stephanie Rodden (11)
Davidson's Mains Primary School

TALE OF TAO

Sapphire eyes, softly blazing,
chocolate-coloured front paws.
Licking his lips in anticipation,
over things he sees and licks and gnaws.

Industrious tail, twitching idly,
lashing from side to side.
As dark as chocolate,
swaying with all his pride.

Wheat-coloured fur,
chocolate-coloured paws and tail.
Bright blue coloured eyes,
to see him there you cannot fail.

Miriam Sakram (11)
Davidson's Mains Primary School

BEAR HUNT

I am lying in the grass.

I see a robin nesting in the tree.
I see animals coming around to greet me.

I hear leaves rustling on the branches.
I hear a gust of wind swiftly blowing past me.

I smell damp bark from the pine trees.
I smell wood smoke burning in the distance.

I feel the bite marks from the bear fight.
I feel blood trickling down my back from the wounds.

Greg Summers (11)
Davidson's Mains Primary School

THE INDIAN CAMP

As we walk through the never-ending woods,
I feel my wounds paining me,
But as my leader looks up in alert,
I forget that feeling and I am jubilant.

Now my body is realising what Luath was encountering,
The smell of smoke means fire,
Fire suggests food,
Rushing into the clearing,
Not thinking what I am doing,
Just my thought of reaching humans.

As I waddle towards the blazing fire,
Humans do come into my focus,
My heart is full of warmth.

My approach is welcome
And greeted with a pat,
Which brings back memories.

People laughing, laughing at me,
I think,
Let's try and impress them more,
But where are Luath and Tao?
Seeing Luath stiff on a rock,
I can hardly recognise him.

A bark meets my ear,
A bark like a shot of lightning,
I am alert once more,
But as I leave, with a heavy heart,
My new friends wish me
A good journey.

Yannick Onifade (11)
Davidson's Mains Primary School

THE HIDDEN CABIN

Their journey is long
but Luath carries on. His friends
trudging behind him.

The cat springs
from fence to bush.
Sometimes slow, sometimes fast.
Not caring where they are going.

A cabin appears
through the trees.
The smell of meat is clear.
A man walks towards them.

'Hello,' he says,
looking at them with a friendly glare.
'Do come in,
I've been expecting you.'

Into the cabin they go,
wishing their happiness showed.
Sitting on the floor
from his command.

The man is queer,
the food is there,
but reachable it is not.
They sit starved on the cold floor.

Since they don't eat,
the man thinks it is time for them to go.
He escorts the dogs to the door.
Their journey carries on with hunger.

Cheryl Lonsdale (11)
Davidson's Mains Primary School

OLD BODGER

The scent of wood smoke
The chatter of the Indians
Suddenly I realised this was my world!
Trotting forward determinedly
My old, unseeing eyes failed again
Using my faithful old nose
To take me in the direction . . .
Of that tantalising smell . . .

Knowing there was food,
Wonderful, glorious food,
A fragrant compound of . . .
Roasting rice,
Wild duck stew
And wood smoke.
I knew this was the place for me.
I also knew we couldn't stay.

I was straining to see,
The place that was made for me.
I could vaguely make out six or seven fires.
Humans meant
Safety,
Warmth,
Food.
Only if they gave it to us easily.
I knew they would.

Hayley Edwards (11)
Davidson's Mains Primary School

THE FIGHT OVER BODGER

I see the Siamese cat as his little brown paws
leap for the coal-black bear,
scratching the bear's black eyes, turned red,
full of anger.

I hear the bear, still in fury, giving a mighty roar,
but this cat is proud and determined.
He still goes on, frantically scratching.

The bear flees further and further into
the dark, dark forest.

I smell the smell of peace and relief,
as the cat, exhausted, staggers towards his friends.
Out of breath, he sits beside Bodger, falling asleep.

I feel so optimistic for the cat,
once out-weighed,
now as tough as a Minotaur.

I think after the cat has eaten,
his resources will be renewed.

Gary Whiting (12)
Davidson's Mains Primary School

LUATH, THE LABRADOR

Luath is a Labrador retriever
Long, soft, reddish-gold coat
So thick it's totally waterproof
His eyes are big and golden-brown
He has a thick protective layer of skin around his neck.

David Ritchie (11)
Davidson's Mains Primary School

COLLIE DOG RUN

Lost in the forest, we come to a farm,
I see chickens that I like to eat,
All juicy and sweet.
I see a man coming out with a gun,
I hear shouting and bawling,
The gun is loaded.

I hear a dog barking,
The farmer lets him out.

I smell danger
Coming fast,
The dog is ready to charge at us.

I feel scared,
My legs are frozen to the spot.

I think we must fight for survival.

We are running away with food in our mouths,
Our tails wagging with delight.
Back to the woods we go,
A lucky escape.

Michael Ranken (11)
Davidson's Mains Primary School

CLOSE SHAVE TAO

I see Tao slip and slide
I see Tao falling from side to side
I hear Tao dash and splash
I hear Tao scratch and catch
I smell the fear, his appalling fear
I think he will try, but then he might die.

Allan Walker (11)
Davidson's Mains Primary School

DANGER

Nothing but the swirling water,
Whirling around.
Rocks everywhere, trying to grab onto them.
The water roaring around me,
Roaring with the whistling wind.
My own cries for help,
Above the whooshing of the water,
Fading away.
Thinking only of what may happen.
Am I going to die or not?
Where, oh where are my two friendly companions?
Seeing only my chocolate paws,
Trying to paddle towards a rock.
Hearing the splashing of my paws in the water.
Thinking of my owner sitting, fishing,
Thinking we're at home!
I see, I hear, I think . . .
Danger!

Jade Mason (11)
Davidson's Mains Primary School

THE BEAR IN THE WOOD

Eyes like blue marbles that glitter and glance,
Pink, springy paws that pounce and then prance.
A growl in his throat like an angry command,
A roar, with pain and a clawed, ugly hand.
A smell of raw flesh and an ocean of blood,
I feel a sharp pain and I'm covered in mud.
I think now there's some hope and the sun starts to shine,
Warmth in my mind with a joy that is mine.

Natalie MacKinnon (11)
Davidson's Mains Primary School

THE LUCKY ESCAPE

As I see the deadly porcupine
I feel a tear in my eye
Knowing it is wrong, I cannot help myself
Following it everywhere.
The hair on my spine begins to prick up
My golden brown eyes look at him.
Then,
As soon as I go for it,
Snap!
In the side of my face
I see a splash of porcupine spikes

Running, running, howling, trying to find help
Slowing down, I see a man.
Great! Saved!
Then I hear a shout
'Get bird!
Get bird! Get bird!'

Entering the house I see Bodger
Hearing, 'Here boy, here boy.'
I walk to the man
Trusting that soon I will be out of pain

He pours whisky on my cut
Then pulls out the spikes
Free at last from pain.

Soon our incredible journey can be completed.

Steven Cameron (11)
Davidson's Mains Primary School

BODGER SENSES HUMANS

Some lights in the distance.
Many fires and smoke.
Voices and laughter that belong to humans.
The crackle of fire like the crackle of walking on leaves.
The delicious, tantalising smell of duck stew,
That makes my mouth water.
Hungry and exhausted because I have been walking miles,
Without any food.
Humans might give me food if I am good.
I must go to them.

Siobhan Doig (11)
Davidson's Mains Primary School

TAO, THE SIAMESE CAT

Crystal, sapphire eyes,
gleaming with curiosity and anticipation.
The Siamese cat's glossy body shines like
a bronze platter in the sunshine.
His chocolate-coloured paws,
washing methodically behind his ears.
His black masked face and cool detached looks
make him a rare beauty,
suited to any occasion.

Abeer Rehan (11)
Davidson's Mains Primary School

CAT SENSES DANGER AHEAD

I see the grass swaying, I see the trees
Blowing gently in the breeze as I stroll past.

I hear the wind whistling,
As if it's telling me something.

I hear my body shivering, scared.

I feel a strange, large presence following me.

I think something is approaching me.

I feel utmost danger.

I wish my friends were here.

There, standing before me is a vicious, ferocious lynx.

Michael Addy (11)
Davidson's Mains Primary School

TAO

Her eyes are like saucers, sapphire-coloured.
With her chocolate-coloured paws,
A puffy, creamy tail,
Her black masked face like a dark room.
Monkey hind legs,
She has a detached look.
With her high ear-splitting screams -
Scare the living daylights out of you.
She is always tense and ready,
While catching a fish she's licking her lips in anticipation.
She is very friendly, never scared.
She puts friends and family first.

Danielle Christina Inglis (11)
Davidson's Mains Primary School

BODGER THE ENGLISH BULL TERRIER

I see Bodger, a very strong dog,
His almond-shaped eyes glitz in the dark.
I see his rough hair bristling in the wind,
His long tongue hanging out while he runs.

He stands there on four sturdy legs,
I hear him panting heavily,
He has run a long distance,
He lies down for a rest,
Then falls asleep with his pink tongue lolling.

He wakens and stands up,
His whip-tapered tail swinging from side to side,
He knows another day is ahead.

Stephanie Cant (11)
Davidson's Mains Primary School

TAO'S IN TROUBLE

The lovely, shiny, blue river,
The rocks everywhere, large ones, small ones.
The sound of the trees, rustling their leaves nearby.
Animals in the trees and on the ground.

The smell of burning reaching my nose,
Making me think constantly of my stomach.
I'm really sad not seeing Tao,
My owner thinking I'm lying in my bed.

As the water moves fast along the river bank,
It sounds like it is roaring loudly
Or like twigs and branches
Hitting each other and the rocks.

Ashley Carse (11)
Davidson's Mains Primary School

TAO AND THE RIVER

Tao's leap of faith had failed,
A goner truly he must be,
For a cat takes to water like a fly to a spider,
As he goes on the river, it's getting wider and wider
And now the dogs have lost a companion,
With the hunter gone, the task becomes insurmountable.

With the dogs trooping on,
The cat in their mind going, then gone.
But they will never forget their true friend,
That remained together with them to the end.
But when Tao hit the waterfall,
It looked like a young girl's cat was lost forever.

But after time the cat was found,
Taken in by a warm-hearted family,
That after weeks he gained his strength
And prepared for a journey about to commence.

Over the hills and far away,
The dogs were gradually going on their journey.
But then they saw a cat, they were very excited,
When they saw it, it was Tao, they were delighted,
For now the trio were together again
And the incredible journey across Canada had started once again.

Ewen Lowrie (11)
Davidson's Mains Primary School

BODGER

Bodger's translucent, slanted, almond eyes,
Sunk deep within their pinkish rims.
Sat on his haunches with his long pink tongue
From his grinning mouth,
Amusing children from the south.

Mr MacKenzie found him at the right time,
Bodger was about to flip the dime.
Mr MacKenzie helped him recover,
But Bodger was still as weak as jelly,
He needed some food inside his belly.

Martin McConnell (11)
Davidson's Mains Primary School

THE DROWNING OF TAO

As I walk across the unsteady stones
Hurting, Bodger begins to move.
My legs start to shake
And the logs start to break.
I don't want to die,
What shall I do?

Slowly my claws start to take grip,
I begin to wobble like a sinking ship,
Nearer and nearer I come to the end,
My head is spinning, going round in a bend.

Near the end, suddenly, I fall
And bang my head.
The water is getting stronger,
It seems to be growing longer.

I wash up on the shore and choke up most of the water,
I think I have a fever,
My head is getting hotter,
When will this ever end?

Gregg Cameron (11)
Davidson's Mains Primary School

THE JUMP

The dam was the only way,
But it was broken in the middle.
I'd have to jump to join my friends,
It was like a terrible riddle.

Will I leap over the water?
I think I should.
Will I make it?
I could, I could.

I made it to the other side,
But soon the logs gave way.
I fell into a deep sleep,
In the river I'd hate to stay.

I wasn't sure what happened that day.
A girl found me in a stream.
I liked living with her,
It was like a dream.

She was kind,
She fed me real food.
But I had to leave,
Although it was rude.

My friends are a-waiting,
Home is my way,
Unfortunately for her and I,
I cannot, really cannot stay.

Jamie Gilchrist (11)
Davidson's Mains Primary School

THE MIRACLE

The beautiful, sparkling, blue river,
it's flowing gently down the banks.
The sounds of birds in the trees
and hives full of bumblebees.

The smell of fire catches my nose,
it makes me think of rabbit and fish.
I feel like I really want to be home,
thinking of my owner all on his own.

The water ahead is as still as a rock,
but for now it's moving swiftly and rapidly.
As if there was a storm ahead,
waiting to catch me and make me dead.

Melissa Pitkeathly (11)
Davidson's Mains Primary School

THE CROSSING

I was still dripping wet from crossing it, the river.
Bodger was just emerging from the cold clutches of it, the river.
Tao was scrambling up and down its banks, the river.
He paused before clambering along it, across it, the river.
The water started to overflow,
Branches started to break away and travel down it, the river.
The next wave of water smashes the dam,
Washing Tao away down it, the river.
Just one look in the young cat's eyes, could tell its distress,
Before being swallowed up by . . . the river.

Ewan Murdoch (11)
Davidson's Mains Primary School

HELP ME, I'M DROWNING

I see a large pond
Right in front of me.
Dogs are able to cross easily,
I see danger, I'm too frightened to cross.

I walk down the edge of the bank,
Look – there is a shorter crossing!
The dogs are determined to help me but I'm not so sure,
I jump and fall and am pulled away.

I try to grab out for a branch,
I miss, I am almost unconscious,
I land on a rock.

I lie until a girl finds me,
Amazingly we make friends,
She helps me recover and
Gives me food,
Delighted I am.

I am safe but I need to find the dogs,
Now I am well again, I must be off.

Graham Sless (11)
Davidson's Mains Primary School

OLD BODGER

Bodger, Bodger lying on the floor,
Every night sleeping by the door.
His heavy head hanging all day.

Bodger, Bodger is very old,
On this journey he is tired and cold.
An elderly, battered dog.

Bodger, Bodger with a stumbling walk,
Summons up the energy to stalk
His prey, too tired to carry on.

Bodger, Bodger determined to find,
Proving he is very caring and kind,
Intelligent and friendly.

Nicolle Carswell (10)
Davidson's Mains Primary School

THE LOST CAT

Tao the Siamese cat,
Chocolate-coloured front paws.
Tao the funny, clever cat,
He opens all the doors,
Latches and doorknobs.
Blue, blazing eyes,
His lips as red as lipstick.
His tail puffed up,
His ear-splitting scream sprang
And monkey hind legs.

Lovely warm coat,
Lashing his tail from side to side.
Tao has a cool detached look.
Illustrious tail twitching idly,
A rare and beautiful enigma,
Swift and efficient traveller.

Leigh DeRighetti (12)
Davidson's Mains Primary School

RUSH OF BLOOD

I see the bear
And I know that I,
I'm in for a scare.

The bear comes around
And my heart starts to pound.

I know the bear is best
And I am gasping for a rest.

Here comes the cat,
As fluent as a bat.

The bear looks queer,
But the cat has no fear.

The bear swipes with all its might,
Meanwhile the cat jumps in flight
And releases a bite.

The fight is over,
I need a rest,
It's for the best.

Nick Anderson (11)
Davidson's Mains Primary School

TAO, THE CAT

Tao, chocolate-coloured paws
With lovely sapphire eyes
Tao would open all doors
Latches and doorknobs
But defeated porcelain handles

Tao loved to clean himself
Behind his ears
Tao also had a chocolate-covered tail
That was puffy
When he smells food
He would lick his lips in anticipation.

Dionne Scott (11)
Davidson's Mains Primary School

TAO, THE CAT

So charming
Tao the cat
Not too skinny
Not too fat
Eyes of blue
Never despise
Never to fear
All noises I hear
A lovely shade of brown
With pointy ears

Brilliant at jumping
Catching my prey
Can I have something different
Every day?
Catching birds
Other beasties
The world so small
Love it all
Every moment
Every minute bit.

Jade Rutherford (11)
Davidson's Mains Primary School

TAO IS TOP

A slick moving Siamese cat
With paws of chocolate sauce.
Good for running on soft grasses
Or even hardened moss.
A thickened coat, the king of cats
Waltzing in our midst.
But a heart of gold who
Adores hugs from kids.
When inhospitable animals attack my friends,
I snarl and hiss in murderous spook,
My tail pricks up, not even a crook.

A black masked face with sapphire eyes,
Banshees scream,
Whiskers in a silver gleam,
With claws of jaunty stature,
The kind that slaughter.
Braver than another cat until I come to
Water!

Carol Moir (11)
Davidson's Mains Primary School

THE BEAVER DAM

I see an old beaver dam where a cat is attempting to cross,
It leaps up into the air and as it lands, there's chaos.
The logs shift, the branches break, the dam begins to move,
I hear the cat screeching as its grip is starting to loosen.
The river current is speeding up,
The cat is nearly drowned,
The logs are crashing, falling,
Making a roaring sound.

The cat's now underwater,
Desperately trying to get some air.
It is struggling to the top,
There are branches everywhere.
The water is calming down,
The cat is nearly dead,
But unknowingly, further down the river,
Help is at hand.

Emma Patrizio (11)
Davidson's Mains Primary School

TAO THE MAGNIFICENT

Tao has sapphire eyes,
Blue and blazing.
His paws are chocolate-coloured,
His face black-masked,
Tao's illustrious tail twitches idly,
His hind legs, monkey-like.

He is as quick as lightning, sharp and smart.
With a fear of water he is still very tough.
A greedy little cat, searching constantly for food.
Mostly happy on his journey.
He likes everything for himself.

He feels that he has to get home,
Home to his family,
His loving owner.

Tao cares about the other two,
The dog called Luath
And the other dog, Bodger.
They belong together.

Alanna Swan (11)
Davidson's Mains Primary School

THE CAT SUPPOSEDLY DROWNED

I see the cat at the other side of the river,
I see the deep, tough river crashing on the rocks,
I hear the cries of the cat as he falls in the river,
I hear the water crashing and bashing against the rocks,
His eyes look cold and frightened.

I see the cat struggle as he crashes between the rocks,
I see the cat halfway across the deep river,
I hear the dog barking, encouraging the cat,
I hear the cat cry in fear.

I see, farther up the river, logs are falling,
I see the cat clinging to a rock, clinging for his life,
I hear the logs crashing towards the cat,
The cat looks terrified and cold.

I see the cat being swept away by the logs,
I see the cat being pushed under the water,
I hear the cat cry and a dog barking,
The cat has been swept away.

Kris Whiting (12)
Davidson's Mains Primary School

THE BLACK NIGHTMARE

A huge, towering bear,
The large, powerful jaws.
A low growling roar, like thunder,
The pounding of gigantic claws.
A hideous odour coming my way,
The claws of death, cutting into my shoulder,
A bright light racing towards me.

A cat, racing to my rescue,
The dog coming too.
A growl of pain,
The bear retreating.
The scent of blood from the cub.
The fear of death, receding.
The world at peace again!

Danielle Maher (11)
Davidson's Mains Primary School

TAO, THE FRIENDLY CAT

My name is Tao, I am a cat,
I love to eat delicious rats,
I have silky, soft, sparkly fur,
When people stroke me, I always purr.

My tail moves swiftly from side to side,
My sapphire-blue eyes are really quite wide.
My paws are brown,
My face is black,
I think I'm quite cute,
Everyone knows that.

I am so lively and happy too,
I am inquisitive, I know that as well as you.
I am very clever,
I am very smart,
I can catch fish
And that's just the start.

Jade Knox (11)
Davidson's Mains Primary School

BEAR FIGHTING

As tired as a hibernating mouse,
Bodger lay there still.
Out of the blue some bear cubs appeared,
Playing deliriously with him.

Noises in the distance came closer to him.
A colossal mother bear approached Bodger,
With blasphemous eyes.

Leaping into the air, the cat pounced onto the bear
And scratched frantically.
His sapphire eyes glared into the bear's with venom.
Never before had he fought so ferociously against an enemy like this.

He escaped without injury, happy to help his friend.

Natasha Todd (11)
Davidson's Mains Primary School

TAO

Tao has dark, sapphire eyes,
A dark mask, the colour of coal,
A black tail and paws the colour of chocolate
And a coat which is black
And it is also thick.
Monkey-like hind legs,
Give her lightning-quick reflexes.
A sharp and inquisitive nose
Helps Tao to smell prey.
Big, sharp ears,
Help Tao hear prey and other animals.
Such an amazing cat.

Grant McPhillips (11)
Davidson's Mains Primary School

LUATH

With my golden fluffy coat
And my deep brown eyes,
I'm sure you'd recognise me.

My teeth sharp and white,
My ears soft and floppy.
My tongue as pink as a flamingo,
Calling for food,
Glorious food,
But I'll have to wait for now.

My legs are long, strong, but thin,
My body weak and hungry for food.
It feels as if it is wearing away,
As tired as anything, my eyes slowly drop,
Tomorrow shall be a bigger day.

Kirsten Simpson (11)
Davidson's Mains Primary School

MY DEFYING LEAP

Swirling blue, cold water under
The brown sticks and logs
Moving inch by inch by the wind
The still water going slowly down the stream
The trees whistling above me
Something dangerous is going to happen
But I take my chance
Feeling as if an ice cube was running down my spine
Ever so slowly
In my mind I'm going to make it
But my senses are not that sure.

Emma Whiting (12)
Davidson's Mains Primary School

CROSSING THE RIVER

We wait, our leader swimming ahead,
I cross, bringing with me dread
And as I go, I see a sight,
A wave hurtling towards me with all its might.

As I go under,
I stare and wonder,
Why they didn't warn or shout or bark,
Why I'm drowning, now it's going dark.

I'm floating, floating, I wonder why?
I cannot see the pure blue sky
And as I float, I see a face,
A dainty child full of grace.

She calls her father, kind-hearted and warm,
Together they nurse me back to health,
If love were money they would have great wealth.

I know that I am almost deaf,
But it's a better fate than certain death,
The water's clogging up my ear,
I know that soon I must leave here.

On a cold night I know her heart is breaking,
Though the road I must be taking,
To my friends, I must travel,
As the way to home, Luath has unravelled.

James Greenhalgh (11)
Davidson's Mains Primary School

MY SENSES

I see a shadow creeping up on me,
I see a cat's shadow creeping up on me.

I hear the steps of the lynx
Approaching, coming towards me.
I hear the lynx, growling,
Footsteps getting louder.

I smell foul smells from the cat's mouth.

I feel as if ice is going down my back.

I think I should run
Before . . . *bang!*
The lynx is almost on me.

I see a thin tree, I run up it,
I see the lynx climbing up the same tree.

I hear the lynx approaching,
Even closer,
I hear the lynx's nails
Scratching the tree.

I smell fear coming, ever so close.

I feel terrified as the lynx gets onto the same branch as me.

I think I'll jump off and run for my life.

Sidrah Ahmed (11)
Davidson's Mains Primary School

A Command From The Top, Bodger Can't Cope

Being dragged along, blistering feet, his long tongue lolling.
His head heavily hanging from his old, battered body.
After his stumbling walk, he sat on his haunches,
As he exhaustedly panted for breath.
His slanted, almond-shaped eyes sunk deep within their pinkish rims.
This downright ugly dog kept a grinning mouth,
As he is pulled through the unknown wilderness surrounding them.
The deep-chested, stocky body and his whip-tapered tail,
Were beginning to disappear, showing that he had not eaten in days.
This honourable breed was not bred to be a traveller,
As it was an unyielding fighter.
His eyes veiled and unseeing,
Being commanded to go.

Shaun Young (11)
Davidson's Mains Primary School

The Indian Encampment

Blackness,
Nothing but blackness.
Laughter in the distance,
Means humans.
Sizzling fires suggests
Food, glorious food.
The tantalising smell of
Wild duck makes my eyes water.
A feeling of happiness
Rushes in here.
I love to be among humans.
What a relief!
Food once more.

Scott Headley (11)
Davidson's Mains Primary School

OLD BODGER

Most people take a glance and see an ugly dog,
Yet in his prime the terrier was a white beauty.
A coat as white as snow,
Eyes as black as coal.
A tail like a little whip,
Short, stubby legs
Holding up a round, stocky body.
Loving the affection of humans
And being the centre of attention.
The dangerous long journey across Canada,
Without humans, must be insurmountable
For this old bull terrier.

Finlay Barron (11)
Davidson's Mains Primary School

TAO'S TALE OF TERROR

The other side of the river,
Sparkling water underneath my aching paws.
The sound of my old companions on the other side,
The water trickling through the beaver dam.
I feel like a tightrope walker,
Attempting to walk over a boiling lake of lava
Or a pit of sharks.
Smelling jeopardy as I wait to cross
The ice-cold water below me.
I am not only going to be sick,
But I'm about to lose one of my nine lives today.

Ailsa McGregor (11)
Davidson's Mains Primary School

TAO

Tao is a Siamese cat with sapphire blue eyes
Which gaze at the sun.
He sits on the floor washing methodically behind his ears.

He sits at the window for hours, lashing his tail from side to side.
A long, thick coat of chocolate colour on his monkey-like hind legs.
He likes to lay curled up in a ball next to the fire.
He is able to open locks, doors and latches.
He's beautiful and proud.

He climbs to the top of a tree and never gets stuck.
He has a banshee scream, so loud you want to cover your ears.
He's warm, cuddly and kind.
I wish I had a cat like that.

Alexandra Graham (11)
Davidson's Mains Primary School

BODGER

Bodger is a dog who is deep-chested and short-tempered,
He has shaped eyes like a Chinese person.
He is really ugly in the face, that's because he's a bull terrier.
Bodger has an elderly body and veins stick out,
He is not a fighter, he always sticks up for himself.
Bodger is a strong fighter but doesn't like fighting.
Bodger stumbles when he walks and he is very slow.
His eyes are veiled and unseeing.

Riccardo Binanti (11)
Davidson's Mains Primary School

THE INCREDIBLE JOURNEY OF TAO, THE SIAMESE CAT

Tao, the Siamese cat,
His eyes so blue they look like sapphires.
His paws like chocolate,
His face so black.
His lovely tail slashing from side to side.
He looks like a rare and beautiful enigma,
A swift and efficient traveller.
His spare-looking eyes watching you
And his soft fur feels like a giant patch of feathers.
Always thinking what he'll find behind every door and window
And always thinking he'll get home, home glorious home.

Rebecca Grant (11)
Davidson's Mains Primary School

TAO, THE SIAMESE CAT

Tao, the Siamese cat with his chocolate-coloured front paws
And his sharp sapphire eyes
With little, pointy ears like a pin
He has monkey-like legs
A detached look and hod thickening coat
With his illustrious tail twitching idly
He spits in murderous devilry
He can scream like a banshee
His sideways movement like a sidewinder snake.

Nicky Mackay (11)
Davidson's Mains Primary School

TAO

Tao is a Siamese cat,
His black masked face with deep sapphire eyes
That blaze bright-blue like the sea.
His anger is like a lion,
Spitting venomously.
A banshee scream
That could ensnare the senses.

Silky front paws coloured chocolate
And dark monkey-like hind legs,
With lethal claws as black as coal
And a twitching tail with a crooked end.

He is as proud as a lion
And as intelligent as could be.
His cool, detached look makes him a beautiful cat.

Danielle Bethune (11)
Davidson's Mains Primary School

BODGER

Bodger with his slanted almond-shaped eyes, engraved with pink rims
And a downright ugly face
He has a sharp grin and a goat-like structure
He is deep-chested with a sharp whipped tail
His pair of pointed ears like devil's spikes
He is an unyielding fighter who never gives up
And a total devoted pet.

Christopher Henry (11)
Davidson's Mains Primary School

BODGER, THE ENGLISH BULL TERRIER

Bodger is an English bull terrier,
He is a downright ugly dog.
Bodger sits proud,
He is a devoted pet.
He gets caught in the light of fire,
It is like he is translucent,
His grinning mouth and his lolling pink tongue,
Large triangular ears like pyramids.

Bodger is generally falling down because he is tired and hungry,
His head hanging down.
Bodger goes to sleep in his bed,
His big brown eyes droopy.

Michael Hamilton (11)
Davidson's Mains Primary School

BODGER, THE ENGLISH BULL TERRIER

Bodger's slanted almond-shaped eyes
Sunk deep within their pinkish rims,
His ears are like pyramids, large and triangular.
His long tongue is as pink as sugar cane.
His grinning mouth stands out.
When his coat gets caught in the sunlight,
His coat almost becomes translucent.
He is a downright ugly dog.

Bodger's got a deep-chested, stocky body,
Gently falling over.
He is hungry and tired.
He is an unyielding fighter and he will never give up.

Craig Anderson (11)
Davidson's Mains Primary School

BODGER

Bodger is an English bull terrier,
His slanted almond-shaped eyes
Sunk into his goat-like body.
His whip-tapered tail bouncing
Off his small, thin legs.
Bodger is downright ugly
And he is always panting,
Everywhere he goes.

Bodger is a devoted pet,
A dog that always obeys his master.
A dog that never gives up,
He always tries his best.

Bodger is old and quiet
And deep-chested.
He is always tired
Because he is so exhausted.
A useless fighter
Because he is so weak.
Bodger walks with his head hung low
And his stumbling walk.

Robyn Burns (11)
Davidson's Mains Primary School

BODGER

His slanted almond-shaped eyes sunk into their pinkish rims.
His long rolling tongue drinking the water.
His small, white ears sticking up – listening to the birds in the trees.
As he walks, his head is down and his paws are dragging along the
Ground because he is too tired from walking so far.
As he is walking, he pants exhaustedly.

Melissa Currie (11)
Davidson's Mains Primary School

BODGER

Bodger with slanted almond-shaped eyes and a battered body
He's downright ugly
Falling along the way home
His long pink tongue hanging from his mouth

A devoted pet
He is an unyielding fighter
He has a chesty, stocky body
One large triangular ear listens for places
But he is a magnificent specimen to look at

He has an elderly, battered body
And generally stumbles when he walks
He has a big, grinning mouth
His teeth are like spikes.

Kyle McLeod (11)
Davidson's Mains Primary School

BODGER

Bodger is an English bull terrier,
He has slanted almond-shaped eyes,
Downright ugly dog.
Bodger does not feel lonely, he feels proud,
Two large, triangular ears,
A long, pink tongue lolling and a grinning mouth.
Bodger is a type which will not give up,
He would keep going.
He loves everyone who shows him love.

Danielle Stevenson (11)
Davidson's Mains Primary School

BODGER

Bodger, slanted, almond-shaped eyes
Sunk deep within their pinkish rims.
His long, pink tongue lolling through the water.
Two large, triangular ears sticking up,
Listening to the birds,
Whip-tapered tail wagging about.
Bodger's deep chest is pumping faster every minute,
His paws are dragging on the ground,
But his head is up, looking around.

Gary Notman (11)
Davidson's Mains Primary School

MY MUM

My mum is a sausage sort of mum,
A 'tidy your room' kind of a mum
A mashed potato in gravy

She is a work hard
Playful,
Ironing,
Cuddling
Kind of mum

She helps me if I am stuck,
Does chores for me,
Makes my food,
Takes me shopping,
Gives me money kind of mum

Actually I love my mum.

Kyle Finlayson (9)
East Craigs Primary School

I HAD A DREAM

I had a dream that the world was made of chocolate,
The trees were made of candy,
The grass was made of liquorice,
The water would be lemonade,
It would be fun.
I would eat all the houses,
I would eat all the trees,
I would eat all the grass
And drink all the water.

Kirsty Ewing (9)
East Craigs Primary School

TWOS

Lots of things come in twos -
Ears and earmuffs, feet and shoes,
Ankles, shoulders, elbows, eyes,
Heels and shins and knees and thighs,
Gumboots, ice skates, mittens, socks,
Humps on camels, hands on clocks
And heads on monsters also do -
Like that one . . .
Hiding right behind you!

Rebecca Challoner (9)
East Craigs Primary School

MY MUM

My mum is a spending sort of mum,
A 'let the cat out' sort of mum,
A huge Yorkshire pudding,
Dough balls,
Mince,
Stobies kind of lady,
She is a clean up,
Ironing,
Dusting,
Polishing,
Put away my clothes
Kind of lady

She helps people when they are hurt,
Is playful,
Tickles me to death,
Makes stuff with me,
Makes me a Pot Noodle.

My mum is a teddy bear mum.

Kirsty Lucas (9)
East Craigs Primary School

SNOWY DAY

When it's snowy I see a white carpet covering the ground
And my frozen breath.
People's cheeks turning red with the cold.
I hear the crunching of my feet as I walk,
I hear the screaming of children
And snowballs hitting the ground.

I feel the cold frost on my cheeks
And my nose is like a cherry.
My ears and my fingers go numb,
I get a chilly shiver down my back.
I smell the crisp air.
When I stick my tongue out,
I taste the icy, frozen flakes trickling down my throat.

Robert Gillespie-Fairbairn (9)
East Craigs Primary School

PET ALIEN

I've got a pet alien
But please don't tell my mother
She'll ground us for a year
Me and my brother

We feed him with the cat's food
We take him to school
We always walk there
Our bags are heavy and full

He helps us with our homework
He always gets the answers right
He does look a wee bit strange
But he is so bright

I've got a pet alien
Who likes to steal
The secret is to
Never be revealed.

Amy Stuart (8)
East Craigs Primary School

THE FISH

I swim in a tank,
With my pal, Frank.
My owner, Jay,
Comes to feed me,
Not a seed,
But instead,
A cosy bed.

For I am a fish,
I have one wish,
My stinky Frank,
Who really stank
Could go away,
So I could play
With myself,
Yes, on a shelf.

I'd have a band,
Where drummers stand
All in a row
And then to mow
My grass like hair,
But then of course,
My tank's force,
Course my tank's force
Could not stand
A little band.

Oh no, the steam,
Forget my dream,
For I am dying, yes today.

Keith Clydesdale (9)
East Craigs Primary School

THE GIANT OF DREAMS

Down in the forest,
A frightening, eerie place,
With shadowy figures
And spooky noises.

By the darkest place,
In the forest so huge,
There he sits,
As quiet as a mouse.

A silent figure,
A lonely, friendless giant,
With nobody to talk to,
In the forest of darkness.

At twelve o'clock quick,
He rushes away,
To a beautiful land,
The land of dreams.

Although you are near,
The giant of sleep,
You will never hear,
The lonely giant.

For the giant can make
Other people follow him,
To the land of the dreams.

They are happy
In the land of dreams,
But they have to go back,
At the coming of light.

Shabana Ahmad (11)
Leith Walk Primary School

SLEEP

Gazing from her castle window
Into the dark forest
Where children's nightmares are manifest
She steals them away
And replaces them with dreams

Silently she moves through the forest
Only sound is leaves swaying gently
In the soft breeze

Her elegant dress sways slightly
No shoes upon her small feet
Her tall but plump body
Onto her wrinkled face
Her faint, misty-blue eyes are exploding
With comfort and love

As she gently lies down
On a massive oak tree
She falls asleep
And ends her nightmare of being alone.

Danielle Gracey (11)
Leith Walk Primary School

NIGHT

A lonely figure comes out at night,
Disappears in the light.
A soft and gentle face,
Leading to a safe and tranquil place.

It moves slowly and silently,
Never speaking a word.
Nobody knows if there is someone there,
It's peaceful and quiet in every way.

He lives quietly in the mountains,
By the quiet, calm stream.
Beautiful at first sight,
He only comes out at night.

Richard Kennedy (11)
Leith Walk Primary School

THE CRY OF THE FOX

The fox let out a helpless cry,
How could its mother deny?
She let out a high-pitched bark,
He could not see her in the dark.

As she came nearer to the cage,
She was truly in rage,
A flash of lightning struck,
Rolling, crashing in the sky,
His mother ran as fast as she could,
She was in an angry mood.

Bang! There it was, that awful sound,
Silence fell on the farm,
All in true alarm,
There was a peaceful feel that night,
But the awful thought that the hunter might
Have hit the fox and been left dead,
Nothing was to be said.

The farm was silent for the rest of the night,
Everyone and everything was in fright,
Especially the mother and her young,
They crept off into the night, never to be seen again.

Emma Stempczyk (11)
Leith Walk Primary School

THE MIDNIGHT FOX

A helpless whine
struggled out of the baby fox
it screamed, yelped, whimpered
desperately the cub tried to force itself out

Thunder struck, banging, drumming, crashing
continuously it roared and rumbled
a huge explosion
like the big bang all over again

Bang, boom, crash, the bullet so strong and powerful
it echoed, exploded
and was totally unstoppable
the smoke rose, the smell was unbearable

Silence struck
so quiet
everything seemed dead
like the peacefulness of a graveyard
or the dreadful quietness of a deserted island.

Zoe Jack (11)
Leith Walk Primary School

THE CHILD OF THE NIGHT

Easily she moves with grace,
the child of the night,
a lonely look upon her face,
till she disappears, come light.

Her hair is black and silky smooth,
her eyes are bright with colour,
her clothes are bold and feel like new,
she's unlike any other.

She lives in a forest, glowing with mist,
where the trees whisper her name
and her home is filled with hopes and wishes,
it's never different, it's never the same.

All through the dark she wanders,
giving us her lovely dreams,
though many people ponder,
if she's ever what she seems?

Sarah Higgins (11)
Leith Walk Primary School

NIGHT POEM

Night is a musical boy
Winding notes, winding instruments,
Going through the sea.
Playing music on the way,
Putting people asleep every second of the day.
There's always a faint outline in the sea,
Trying not to be seen.
Casts a spell,
Flitting to his cottage on the island,
Not to be seen.
Working with music,
His life is endless.
One eye green, another blue,
His mouth shaped for all musical instruments.
Hair black, silky but smooth,
His clothing – soft, green fleece.
He speaks all musical sounds.
Lives in a cottage with music and notes.
Night to me is comforting, always.

Hamish Bamford (11)
Leith Walk Primary School

SLEEP

Last night I saw a little girl
She took me to a place
A place where it is dark but safe
Dreams all around her lovely face

The small girl was so peaceful
Her hair was softened gold
The sweetest fairy tale that ever
Could be told

Her eyes blue and gentle
Her face as still as space
She was the most lovely thing
In this dreamland place

She looks so sad and lonely
As if about to cry
But still she doesn't make a sound
And I cannot think why

Soon she starts to fade
To where she did not say
But soon I am awake again
To start another day.

Poppy Sutherland (11)
Leith Walk Primary School

NIGHT

Along a dark, creepy road where the moon rarely shone
Lives a mysterious beggar who never spoke to anyone

His garb was darker than the starlit sky
His eyes were misty blackness
He moves so easily through the filth and muck
Stealing people's lives, sending them to sleep so he can feel alive

In daylight hours he is never seen
Though a shadow is noticed where he wakes at night
The beggar overpowered by day, finally steals the sun
And releases the moon
Waiting for the end of day so the beggar of sleep
Can strike again.

Craig Buckingham (11)
Leith Walk Primary School

NIGHT

In a land of rest and slumber,
there a silver web of dew and dreams,
the green hills go up and under
the winding, twisting, swirling streams.

In the garden of immoral and wrong,
there in the illusional dwelling,
sat a phantom figure singing his song,
in the garden of immoral and wrong.

At night he follows those who enter
the land of rest and slumber,
he casts a sinister spell,
his victims fall under.

But when the sun starts to ascend
in the garden,
he glides back to his sinful residence,
waiting to sing his song.

So anyone who dares to enter,
watch out for the shadowy figure,
for he will snatch the chance
to cast his spell over you.

Evie Thornton (11)
Leith Walk Primary School

DREAMS

On a peaceful hill,
a beach of dreams,
by quiet gardens
and winding streams.

There she sits,
by a lonely tree,
watching the waves
on a silent sea.

Stars shining brightly above,
sweet silence,
except for the wind
and the call of the dove.

A hazy woman,
the forgotten song,
somehow right
yet somehow wrong.

She is a lingering scent,
another place,
a shining star,
she's full of grace

And when we wake,
she is somehow gone,
somehow right
yet somehow wrong.

Ailsa Donaldson (11)
Leith Walk Primary School

NIGHT

Night, a shy, lonely figure,
Night just clicks his fingers,
You will be deep into his dreams.

You see his shiny eyes
From a long distance away,
He talks and talks
As long as you stay asleep.

He appears, slim, small, peaceful eyes,
As you walk closer to him
In the long grassy field,
You get warmer.

As the shadow of the sun comes out,
The lonely figure fades away.

Rumi Ghafoor (11)
Leith Walk Primary School

NIGHT

Night, lord of the underworld,
black, silent, shadowy figure.

Slyly creeping in the hours of dark.

Luring entranced people to the underworld.

Trapping them in dark, dingy caves
slaves of the underworld beings.

He fears only sun and light,
so he only appears at night.

Ewan Gibbs (11)
Leith Walk Primary School

UNHAPPY WOMAN

She swiftly moves through the night,
A shadow in the dark,
A faint figure moving gracefully,
Dancing by the shore.
The waves crash against the dove-grey rocks,
Her voice like the sea, so deep,
Hypnotic voice to a world of rest,
Peacefully to sleep.
Her golden hair like a yellow star,
Her eyes as green as a leaf
And her voice like a call,
Like you cannot hear,
In a silent trance to sleep.
Just the magic in her voice,
Peacefully to sleep.

Erin Quinn (11)
Leith Walk Primary School

JENNY, MY FRIEND

She is bright yellow,
A sunny spring day,
In a big park,
She is a colourful rainbow
And a warm, comfy armchair,
She is a funny friend,
She is a big chocolate cake.

Danielle Jeffery (11)
Leith Walk Primary School

ANGEL CREATURE FROM THE DEPTHS

The dazzling creature glitters and sparkles
The creature in pain would
'Harkle, harkle'.

The angelic creatures, colours,
Greens and pink,
Watch it save as a large boat sink,
It saves the people and takes
Them to a surface above,
Its soft, velvety skin is like
A white dove.

For its babies to eat, it would
Collect plants,
For itself it would collect
About 200 ants.

This dazzling creatures glitters
And sparkles,
The creature in pain would
'Harkle, harkle'.

It has three fins on each side,
Through the sea it would
Splash and glide.

Its hair is long and pale,
You may have heard this in
Granny's tale,
The name is famous,
Angelpale Star.

Emma Cookson-Brown (12)
St Mary's Leith Primary School

CREATURE FROM THE DEEP!

This creature has a scaly skin,
It shimmers in the sun,
Its beautiful face and silky tail,
It can be big but it's not a whale.

It moves like a dolphin and sounds like a bird,
Nobody's seen its face, perhaps in a blur,
If you see it, please tell me,
If it's in a lake or in the sea.

It eats the plants and weeds,
That is how it feeds,
If a predator comes near,
It panics and will not fear.

This animal is brave, bold and strong,
People misjudge this creature, some are very wrong,
As you watch this incredible thing,
You fall into a dream like an unbreakable ring.

Some people say that it's a dangerous thing,
But I know better, it's as gentle as this poem we sing,
There's been researchers in the deep,
Making the creature cry and weep.

Its eyes are like stars,
This creature hasn't seen land or cars,
It lives in the water
And it swims like an otter.

Its habitat is filled with rocks and that's where it hides,
It's like a wave as it glides across the sea or perhaps a lake,
We just be careful not to overtake.

Sometimes this creature is danger,
Sometimes you have to scream,
Hurry, call a doctor,
Because of course, it's the Loch Ness Monster!

Dayna Turnbull (11)
St Mary's Leith Primary School

MONSTER FROM THE DEEP

With its claws like scorpions' stingers,
Its eyes like the sun itself,
Teeth like terrible tarantulas, ferocious but fabulous too,
Its body is a big bag of blubber,
Its feet like spikes of fire that roar,
Down in the ocean blue,
Deep in the ocean dark.

It lurks along the ocean bed and waits for something to come
And when that victim does appear,
It grabs it and chews it like a piece of bubblegum,
Its favourite victim is the mermaid,
With her heart so kind and pure,
It likes the eyes, the tongue and throat,
For those are the monster's favourite lure.

I am afraid to say that this legend is true,
About the monster that lurks down in the ocean blue,
Deep in the ocean dark,
Sad though it may seem,
Unfortunately true,
That this monster could get anything, anything, including *you!*

Fay Butler
St Mary's Leith Primary School

THE SCREECHER

The sailors say,
That on the rocky bay,
Alas it sleeps, the creature,
They called this hideous monster the Screecher.

For it used to come up with its sun-ball tail
And its song like a cry of a whale,
It came up with its sun-ball tail
And the sailors watched with their beaming eyes,
Till it blinds them with beauty and they fall in the water, drown and die.

Until one day one sailor said, 'The girl, the Screecher will pay.'
He got an arrow
And when this beauty arose he threw the weapon,
The hit was narrow.

The creature fell down for the ocean to keep,
Into a long, deep sleep,
The sailors now when they travel are safe,
They are saved from the terrible Screecher.

Ruby Alden-Gibson (11)
St Mary's Leith Primary School

THE OCTO-MERMAID

The Octo-mermaid isn't like you and me,
Her white, sparkling wings glide through the open sea,
She is as good as gold,
As she has been told.

Her personality shines in like the sun,
She's nothing like her evil twin sister, Octo-demon,
She has a blue and red flowered top,
Octo-demon tries to make her head go pop.

She saves the day with the help of her wand,
She feels even better than the famous James Bond,
She saves dolphins, sharks and whales,
As they give a wave to say thank you from their tails.

Another day rests,
But her sister failed the test,
We all get along like best friends.

Tsara Ford (11)
St Mary's Leith Primary School

MEMORIES OF THE MERMAID

Beneath the bubbling, burbling bay,
To the giggling, colourful coral reef.
Her eight turning, terrible tails
Lurk in the sea while sailors sleep.

The massive mermaid with fins like fire,
Crawls to the lightning sky.
She wraps her tails around the boat
And crushes it till the sailors die.

Then with one last ferocious blow,
A boy is tossed into the sea.
A fisherman finds him alive in the morning
And is told how he got away free.

Now the boy is an old man
And tells the story of that dreadful day
And the people rarely go out in the sea,
They don't want to get in the mermaid's way.

Charlotte Martin (11)
St Mary's Leith Primary School

THE MYSTICAL MONSTER

A long time ago there was said to be legends of the two-headed beast,
If caught, treasure would be revealed in the head . . .

The monster lives in the sea,
It comes up at night to feed.

It has strong, white, crunching teeth,
Like the scrapyard crusher.

It spits water out, like a toilet flusher.

It has a big, red scar on its chest,
It never has time to rest.

It is always endangering the sea,
All the other animals just flee.

When sailors go out to capture it,
They are never seen again.

Or they will lie on the abyssal plain,
People are always saying it's a pain.

The army are after the beast,
When they catch it they will have a big feast.

It lurks around the Mediterranean Sea,
Where it is just waiting to feast.

'I'm glad it's not got me!'

Joseph Santangeli (11)
St Mary's Leith Primary School

THE ANIMAL

Deep, deep down,
We have found,
A large kind of animal,
We think that it's a cannibal.

What a mistake,
Now he'll take
Us to the deep.

This horrible, terrible monster,
It sounds like a crying baby,
When we went deep, deep down,
We saw one of the crowns.

What a mistake,
Now he'll take
Us to the deep.

He'll crash us, trash us,
Bash us, kill us,
What will he do next?

What a mistake,
Now he'll take
Us to the deep.

Ivana Coppola (11)
St Mary's Leith Primary School

THE SAILOR SNATCHER

A beautiful creation, a beautiful creature,
But although she is pretty, beware, do not treat her,
Her eyes are narrowed, she licks her lips,
Run you fools! Do not come across this.

Her hair is long and golden, although alas,
Her voice is like an angel and her eyes are blue as glass,
She swims with peaceful strokes and so graceful too,
She will have you under her spell, you and all your crew!

They say that she used to long ago,
Rock the sailors to and fro,
Then quick as a wink and a wave of her hand,
She lulls them to sleep with magical sand.

She whips them down to her underwater lair
And what is underneath will surely give you a scare,
A long, black cave with eels and ocean bats,
Smiley serpents and blood-filled vats.

She has a pot in the middle of the room,
She will make you bathe and writhe in doom,
So run, make haste, don't stop and stare,
She will not change her mind, that's clear!

Beth Benger (11)
St Mary's Leith Primary School

FROM THE MURKY DEPTHS

A bony burgle baggling in the depths
Feeding on a slithery, slimy seth
Long, thin bones, harder than stones
The waves cower upon its roar
While dead derk dags soar

Its tail as sharp as glass
Its hair a grimy tass

From the murky depths, it moves like no other
Between seths who kill each other
The great sword it carries is smashing
Men's bodies are crashing
Boats go crick and crack
A sword goes click and clack

From the murky depths

So the tales go
The merman still wanders in woe
Killing seths
Creating storms in the depths
Till the day it dies
You will always hear its cries
From the murky depths.

Liam Gannon (11)
St Mary's Leith Primary School

PRINCESS MERMAID

Under the water, deep, deep down,
Princess Mermaid swimming about,
Never to be seen,
With her friends she plays,
Scar-ed to come up
And scared to go down,
She swims about, never to be seen,
She helps the people who are hurt,
But she sets a spell,
So they don't realise
That they've seen her,
She lays the people on the beach
And off she goes back down,
Out of reach.

Louise Stuart (11)
St Mary's Leith Primary School

ICNOMINOS HORICON

It is said to be, that under the sea,
The Icnominos Horicon lies beneath,
Its razor-sharp claws and ear-splitting screams,
You could probably not imagine the sting in your wildest dreams.

It catches its food by learning the name of its prey,
Suddenly he's the hunter and you're the meal of the day,
Even if you escape this beast,
It's probably too late, you are the feast.

It is said to be, that under the sea,
The Icnominos Horicon lies beneath.

Joshua Cooper (11)
St Mary's Leith Primary School

DOOM

At the bottom of the ocean you will find dead in mind
At the bottom of the ocean you will find a granny screaming out
of her mind
At the bottom of the ocean you will find someone crying and dying
At the bottom of the ocean you will find the big, ugly *doom.*

Gareth Rutherford-Jones (11)
St Mary's Leith Primary School

THE RIVER

The river is an alligator
Small but fast
Cold jumble of rocks
Comes to steep drop
Crashes down
Carries on its journey

Growing, swelling, slowing
Starting to sway, crashing its massive tail
Off the sides
Wearing away at the bank

Enormous alligator
Much slower than ever before
Picks up lots of stones and dirt
Gathering more and more as it grows

And rushes to the sea.

Joseph Edwards (11)
South Morningside Primary School

THE RIVER

As the night wind swoops and whistles,
The soft tapping sound of this bull breaks.
Flowing simply through its tiny share of the world.
As the journey continues,
This creature is at a very early stage of its life.
Wrestling away at these tiny pebbles further, through the night,
This bull increases its power, pushing itself harder,
Piling on the pressure.
As the battering noise rises,
Ready for the following morning.
This bull is ready for its roughest ride yet.

The roar of the bull sounds, the charge starts,
The thundering noise of rapids and the temper attack.
Battering rocks, shaving the surface, proving its wrath to the world.
Combining and winding away,
The sprinting skills, the accelerating speed, the hacking, attacking.
Nothing has stood in this bull's way
And nothing will.
The desperate bull has fought hard,
Without a care in the world.
Now coming to the end.
The force and hard work is over,
Time to enjoy the relaxing flow.

This wild bull has reached its destiny,
Battering, hacking, forcing,
Now all in the past,
Now time to rest,
Now time to finish the day,
Now on course for the gates of sea.

Duncan Craig (11)
South Morningside Primary School

THE RIVER

The river is a rhino calf,
Newly born and tumbling,
Scraping away at the banks,
Nibbling here and there,
Falling over rocks on new wobbly legs.

The river is a rhinoceros,
Heavy, cutting a valley,
Building up an appetite for banks,
A great hulk, fatter and taller,
Meandering away from the herd,
A healthy adult rhino.

The river is the leader of a herd of rhinos,
Chomping constantly at banks,
Straying back and forward lazily,
New herd members form tributaries,
So much heavier, creating giant valley,
Stampeding in a flood, a mass of thundering feet,
Delta forming where the herd splits.

Stuart Connal (10)
South Morningside Primary School

TEMPTATION

Temptation is a slithering serpent,
Tempting you to steal what you crave
And burn what you hate.
Wrapping you up in a hard, cold, cruel
Blanket of selfishness.

Jenny Clark (10)
South Morningside Primary School

THE RIVER

The river is a human being,
    A baby human being,
Swiftly crawling downhill,
    Gnawing away at the riverbank,
Drooling over a small waterfall.

The river is a human being,
    Middle-aged, wise and steady,
Raging like a flood, flowing downhill,
    Flooding cities, crushing lives,
Meandering back and forth,
    Flowing down a one-way line.

The river is a human being,
    Elderly and tired,
Old, slow and lazy,
    Watching nature go by,
In the last stages of life,
    Flowing out to sea.

Graeme Campbell (11)
South Morningside Primary School

IN MY IMAGINATION

In my imagination I can
Destroy devilish demons with one swift sword strike
Discover diamonds in dwarves' deep dark dungeons
Dual deadly, dangerous dragons till death
But I'm only an ordinary boy

In my imagination I can
Trounce troublesome trolls to Timbuktu
Trace transgressors like terrific Sherlock Holmes
Tame terrible pterodactyls
But I'm only an ordinary boy

In my imagination I can
Do war with warlocks
Wipe out wizard warriors
Wrestle witches with weapons
But I'm only an ordinary boy.

Tom Barrett (10)
South Morningside Primary School

THE RIVER

The river is a dangerous snake,
Slithering quickly around rocks and stones,
Avoiding every tree,
Gnawing away chunks of land,
Young and alert, catching people on the way,
Hiding away every second.

The snake is now an adult,
Growing bigger every minute,
Strong and fierce,
Twisting around, scraping away,
Letting out unwanted waste,
Sometimes meeting a mate,
Then journey on together.

The snake is very angry,
Pours out, flooding villages,
Eating away over land,
Then slowly calms again.

The snake is very old,
Old and slow and very tired,
Eventually arriving at the sea.

Sandy Fok (11)
South Morningside Primary School

THE DOLPHINS

I wait on the beach, look out to the sea,
Then they come, my friends, the dolphins,
Their sleek, smooth, slender bodies,
Wide eyes and tender tails,
Leaping out of the water,
Gliding, swiftly through the air,
Then with a splash they are gone,
But reappear elsewhere,
Singing to all with squeaks and eeks,
I gradually understand their plea,
'Anyone that hunts the sea, leave our kind alone,
We deserve to live our lives,
Not to be caught or killed'.
Then soon the sun goes down and darkness takes over,
My dolphin friends disappear for good,
But I'll be waiting for them tomorrow.

Rebecca Chapman (10)
South Morningside Primary School

ANGER

My anger feels like acid and molten lava,
blended together sweeping through houses and villages.
It looks like a half-demolished ten-storey building,
still burning and spitting.
It tastes like hot chilli peppers,
burning holes in my tongue.
It smells like a skunk trying to protect itself
from its predators.
My anger is a person being executed,
for something he hasn't done.

Anna McGinley (10)
South Morningside Primary School

WIND

Wind, wind, it flies in air,
Swoosh, swash, as it twirls,
It sweeps me off my feet,
It seems like a giant,
As it seems so big
Compared to me,
It whizzes past me
As a train, it curls and curves,
In and out of me like I'm in jail,
Now it seems like I'm
Going through the seasons,
Then stop! The wind drops me in a bench
And carries on with its journey.

Stuart Willder (10)
South Morningside Primary School

THE TEXAS TORNADO

The tornado twisted, turned, whistled
Sucking in and destroying,
People scattered and fled,
Some to shelter but most to death

After the tornado, in debris lay a hopeless wreck
And Texas was no more,
For houses lay as if sleeping,
Crumbling to the Texas floor,
Skyscrapers now floor-scrapers,
A heck of a blow gave the Texas tornado.

Jacob Flapan (10)
South Morningside Primary School

THE FIERCE TIGER

The river is a running tiger,
Chasing its tail round the rocks.
Wagging its tail like little meanders,
Jumping in, making little splashes and hitting off the rocks,
Crunching its prey off the stones,
Freezing cold as the tiger breathes.

Slower and slower as the tiger goes further,
Springs over waterfalls catching its prey,
Bigger meanders growing as it feels happier.

Smashing trees as the flood starts
Meeting a friend at a conference,
Happier, much happier as meanders get bigger,
Meeting the sea and starting to sleep.

James Hall (11)
South Morningside Primary School

IN WINTER

In winter the ground glitters with freshly-laid snow
In winter old men grumble in gruff mumbles as they shovel paths
In winter children laugh as they shoot down hills on their sleighs
In winter the voices of carol singers are sent echoing down streets
In winter snowmen brighten folks' spirits as they pass
In spring the winter has gone, the snow has melted, the snowmen
                                                    are far away
And now we wait for another winter to come . . .

Lisa Liddle (10)
South Morningside Primary School

STARS

Pointed balls of gas,
Millions of miles away,
Shining in the night,
Hidden in the day.

Luminous in the brilliant sky,
Haunting and invisible in the day,
That's the amazing balls of gas,
Millions of miles away.

The stars are like fireflies,
Floating after the day,
When the sun comes up they all scurry away,
Rising again on the next moon,
Ready to hover in the black, blue gloom.

Becky Crook (10)
South Morningside Primary School

SNOW

Snow is like a thick white sheet in wintertime.
Children laugh while throwing snowballs and making snowmen.
Snow is as soft as a newborn lamb's fleece.
People with their sleighs slide down hills.
Snow is like a silver path made overnight.
Carol singers tread in snow making glistening footprints.
The spring comes and winter's far away.

Jessica Williams (10)
South Morningside Primary School

MY SUBMARINE

In my submarine I have swum across the water.
I have glided like a whale.
I have been places where no man has been before.
I have even uncovered some gold and silver.
Then I went to the surface.
There was a big storm, *suddenly!*
I hear,
'Stop splashing me.'
I open my eyes, I saw my mum all wet,
I forgot I was only in my bath.

Megan Hughes (10)
South Morningside Primary School

LOVE

Love is my strength that keeps me going,
Love is a tower I lean on,
It shall never fall,
My love for life and happiness is
Always there to help,
Love is the joy of the world,
Not anything else,
Love should never fade
Because life without love
Is no life at all . . .

Joanne Baker (10)
South Morningside Primary School

AT CHRISTMAS TIME

At Christmas time it's as cold as the moon
But everyone's as kind as the sun
When Santa arrives the presents arrive
And everyone's in a jolly mood
When Christmas arrives your family arrive
And you have a fantastic meal
At Christmas time your excitement crosses the line
And you kiss and hug all day
But after Christmas time you have a boring life
Because you're all back to school.

Alex Honhold (10)
South Morningside Primary School

THE ORCA WHALE

The killer whale, an orca
Is like a cloud drifting through the sky,
But in the ocean, bottomless and dark,
Black and white in colour,
A giant mint humbug,
Floating through the sea,
Gliding through the Pacific,
Searching for sardines, tuna and others,
To catch for its lunch.

Laura Morrison (10)
South Morningside Primary School

MY GARDEN

My garden is like a rainforest
So many trees and plants
All the trees seem so enormous
And plants so unusually strange

My garden is like a rainforest
If I close my eyes I can see a dart frog
A sloth hanging upside down

My garden is like a rainforest
But where are the beautiful, lively humming birds?
I can only see a garden sparrow
And where are the exciting tribes people?
I can only see a rusty, old garden gnome
That's because I'm in my rainforest garden.

Laura Wilson (10)
South Morningside Primary School

DEPRESSION

My depression drowns me in misery,
It draws its prey tight in its strong grasp,
I mumble and grumble in despair,
An angry and hateful voice fills my head,
The sun goes down in my brain,
Depression haunts me like a ghost,
Not pearly-white but as black as night,
Depression makes me feel so small,
But I know I can fight it!

Sarah Maxwell (10)
South Morningside Primary School

MOON

Hidden in the daytime
Shining in the night

Silver, blue and white
In the moon that is so bright

I see calm blue sea
Below a silver path
Shining, waiting for
Someone to cross
Although only the
Reflection of the silver
Moon above.

Josie Morris (10)
South Morningside Primary School

THE LION

The lion's glimmering golden coat,
Beams in the sun's ray,
Like a daffodil on fire,
The mane is like rough rocks,
On the coast of Skye,
The tail swishes and sways,
Like grass in a summer breeze,
He eats a man for dinner,
His legs are quicker than a mouse.

Ben McClellan (10)
South Morningside Primary School

SNOWBOARDING

S is for snow covering the hills
N is for narrowly missing an avalanche
O is for off into snowy hills
W is for waiting for the chairlift
B is for boarding on the slopes
O is for on the jump, flying through the air
A is for agony, breaking your leg
R is for racing on the slope
D is for driving home in your car
I is for in a café on the hill having lunch
N is for nearly falling over
G is for getting sent to hospital.

Tony Stuart (10)
South Morningside Primary School

A GARTER SNAKE

The garter snake has glistening scales
Its red and black tongue flicks out to smell
The heat-sensing pits on the side of its head
Guides it through the dark, silent forest
He hunts on his own, stealthily creeping
Through the silent forest
His patience is unique as it is the only way
To catch his suspicious prey.

Josh McQueen (10)
South Morningside Primary School

I Wish It Snowed Every Day

I wish it snowed every day,
But the wind just blows away,
I think snow is the greatest and the best,
It's better than ice, wind and all the rest.
When I'm lucky, the snow is thick and tall,
Sometimes it's tiny, tender and small.
I make a snowman and my toes have already froze,
I used coal as eyes and a carrot for his nose.

Leigh Kasperek (9)
South Morningside Primary School

Skiing

Up the hill and down the track
Skid at the bottom, it's time to go back
Up and up and up we ride
Off the chairlift and ready to go
It's on with the skis and down the snow
Time to go, 'What! No! No! No!'

Fraser Henderson (10)
South Morningside Primary School

Jaguar In The Jungle

In the dark, green, actionless forest,
The trees 'swish' and the wind
Whistles through the hair of the jaguar,
As she gracefully pounces on a motionless capybara
And gathers it in her long, sharp teeth.

Dianne McKenna (10)
South Morningside Primary School

THE FOOTBALL CUP

In the semi-final of the football cup
Ipswich Town in their regular strip of blue,
Versus Manchester United in their traditional red.

With the fans all eager
And the bookie's money climbing,
The atmosphere was set for the biggest game in town!

I was ecstatically excited,
I couldn't be more delighted
That the football cup semi-final was coming to town!

It's after the game,
We have won by three goals to two
And now we're in the final against . . . oh no, Chelsea!

Jack Kennedy (10)
South Morningside Primary School

TOM WATSON

My cat's name is Puss
My cat is fast as the wind
My cat is always here when I want it
Puss is one of the best things that happened to me
She is cosy as a pillow
She is sharp as wind
And now my cat is dead.

Tom Watson (9)
South Morningside Primary School

FEAR AND DANGER

The fear and danger is crawling up my back
Into my intestine, into my rucksack
It's moving up my body, creaking through my nerves
And when it gets to a certain point, it starts to burn
It's firing through my ears, sneaking through my eyes
And then it just decides to stop before it gets my thighs.

James Mackintosh (10)
South Morningside Primary School

DEAD MAN WALKING

The dead man walking isn't scared
To die in shame on an electric chair
He dives down deep to Hell
He stumbles down to the deep, dark cell
Now the dead man walking is scared.

Amar Singh (10)
South Morningside Primary School

SMALL, SILVER SNOWFLAKE

Small, silver snowflake softly falling down,
Small, silver snowflake, children playing in the town,
Shivering, glittering, smooth as silk,
Small, silver snowflake, glittering, gliding to the ground,
Small, silver snowflake, soft, quiet, nowhere to be found.

Imogen Adderley (9)
The Mary Erskine & Stewart's Melville Junior School

FIREWORKS

They screech all the way up,
To their highest point.
Trailing glitter the whole way,
Then they come streaming down,
While everyone is watching,
Looking amused at the dazzling light.

Catherine wheels spinning round,
As fast as helicopter blades
And as colourful as a rainbow,
All the children are clapping their hands
And telling their friends,
The ones they like best.

Rattling rockets flying up at the speed of light,
Bursting into clouds of colours,
Then floating down as gently as snow falling,
Sparkling in the night sky
And then the light show's over
And the sky is silent.

Adam Hamoudi (9)
The Mary Erskine & Stewart's Melville Junior School

SNOW POEM

Snow fall, slow fall, come down the snowflakes
Let's have fun, grab a hot bun and hold it in case you get cold
Snow fall, slow fall, come down the snowflakes
Snow, snow, nothing better than white, sparkling snow
Snow go slow, snow say goodbye to the white, glittering, sparkling
Snow!

Simon Osborne (9)
The Mary Erskine & Stewart's Melville Junior School

WAR

Screaming, crying, children littering the streets,
Blazing fire roaming the city.
Worried, upset people.
'We wonder why this is happening?'
The baffled people say.

Bombs in the darkness,
Screams of people dying.
The stinking smell of blood.
'We wonder why this is happening?'
The baffled people say.

Wounded in the hut,
Nurses running to and fro.
Rubble on the streets.
'We wonder why this is happening?'
The baffled people say.

Shona Scott (11)
The Mary Erskine & Stewart's Melville Junior School

TORNADO

Tracking down things to destroy,
Swooshing big but not a toy,
Don't go near or else you'll die,
Rampaging, horrible, killing in the sky,
Twisting and turning,
Crashing and destructive.

So never go near to the deadly
Tornado!

Sebastian Mylchreest (9)
The Mary Erskine & Stewart's Melville Junior School

DARK CLOUDS

Dark clouds roll across the sky,
Scaring both you and I.
All the animals in snug homes,
All we have is skin and bones.
Dark clouds roll across the sky,
Scaring both you and I.
Taming the sun, ripping the sky,
Bye-bye sun, bye-bye.
Dark clouds roll across the sky,
Scaring both you and I.
Making the wind howl at home,
North wind, east wind, so and so.
Dark clouds, was that the sun?
No, I must be getting glum.
There's the sun, look now,
Crash, bang, pow.
Oh, more dark clouds roll across the sky,
Scaring both you and I.
Abandon ship, abandon ship,
Time to go home, fly!

Annie Armstrong (9)
The Mary Erskine & Stewart's Melville Junior School

WHIRLWIND

Whirlwind, whirlwind, it comes spinning down
with screams from the roof

It's a spiral of damage, anger disturbs
the houses with spinny circles of destruction

It destroys everything in its path!

Ewan Mitchell (9)
The Mary Erskine & Stewart's Melville Junior School

FIREWORKS

It was a cold winter's night,
All was silent,
Then all of a sudden banging filled the air,
All you could hear was swoosh, bang,
Then a twisting flame of fire
Came out of nowhere.
The crowd went 'Wow!'
A pink, gold and silver dome
Filled the sky, it hovered for a minute,
Then *bang!*
An exploding star faded away,
As a gold firework came up behind it,
I was blinded by its brightness.

Hilary Taylor (9)
The Mary Erskine & Stewart's Melville Junior School

YELLOW BALLOON

The sun,
Why does it shine on us?
Is it to show us beauty, joy or love?
As big as a yellow balloon,
Gravity is no match to this big, yellow balloon.
Its light fills the air,
Its light bulges out, compared to others.
Oh so beautiful it is!
The sun.
The sun has a light so bright,
It goes out at night.

Michael Clark (9)
The Mary Erskine & Stewart's Melville Junior School

FIRE

F ire is fierce, ferocious and frequent.
I t's always outstandingly hot.
R oasting, rumbling, ready to fire.
E verything crumbling in its path.

I ncoming ash-bombs fly into action.
S izzling, hissing, burning like a furnace.

F izzing, whizzing, spitting out ash.
I magine fire, like a fire demon only stopping if it is squashed.
E very tree is being pulled to the ground.
R unning like a river, twisting, turning, never stopping.
C rushing, crashing fire enters town.
E verything's gone now.

Ruairidh Morrison (9)
The Mary Erskine & Stewart's Melville Junior School

THE RAIN

Some people think the rain is fab
Some people think the rain is bad
It makes some people very sad
It makes me very glad
Because without rain all we would have is sun, sun, sun
That makes me very glum
The weather has a strange way of doing
The opposite of what you want
You would like rain one day, but it will give you sun.

Joe McGregor (9)
The Mary Erskine & Stewart's Melville Junior School

FIRE

H issing fire everywhere
I don't know what to do!
S pitting, storming, raging
S pinning round and round
I have to do something!
N oisy, burning, twisting, turning
G etting hotter, getting bigger

F erocious fire!
I don't know what to do!
R uining the village
E ntire belongings, gone.

Lauren Mercer (8)
The Mary Erskine & Stewart's Melville Junior School

THE MONKEY

The monkey swung from tree to tree,
It never stopped to think.
But then it stopped outside a pond
And had a little drink.
It wiped its mouth and swung again,
Until it saw a bird.
Its tail was very pink and brown,
The monkey laughed out loud.
The bird got mad, so very mad,
It pecked him on the head.
The monkey fell and ran away,
He wanted to sleep in bed.

Euan Williamson (9)
The Mary Erskine & Stewart's Melville Junior School

FIRE IS BURNING

F ire starts to spread out far,
I t's burning everything, even cars,
R un for your life before it gets you,
E verything going wrong, what can we do?

I wish I was at home in my swing tyre,
S nuggled, all cosy in front of the fire.

B urning, crackling,
U nsuspected bangs,
R un, run, run for your life,
N ow it's moving through the trees like butter on a knife,
I t's going to get us, that I know,
N ow we have to get down low,
G iving sparks into the air.

I wish, I wish I was not here!

Riona MacGillivray (9)
The Mary Erskine & Stewart's Melville Junior School

THE SUN'S PRISON

Here comes a whiff of smoke
Like a shabby, tatty rag
Stealing the sun away
Seldom the sun peeks out
From its silvery prison
Here comes a whiff of smoke
Slaving the sun away, diminishing
It dies away so the moon can come and play.

Lewis Harding (9)
The Mary Erskine & Stewart's Melville Junior School

RAVAGED BY WAR

The dawn was nigh when it struck,
The smell of fear floods the air,
While crying sirens sail the land,
Evilness has struck our race.

As we cry and plead for rations,
Soldiers try to save our nations,
This cold dreaded war shall not be ended,
Until one man is caught and made guilty.

Everyone suspects this man,
So battle troops hunt him down,
Until he is found, dead or alive,
We shall never be safe.

Kenneth Murdie (10)
The Mary Erskine & Stewart's Melville Junior School

THE TORNADO

Running, twisting, flying through the air,
Some of the people just stand and stare,
All the rest run far and wide,
But the tornado flies like a glide,
All the trees wrecked and broken,
Everybody just stands, mouths wide open,
Soon the tornado disappears,
The people are glad because there's no fear.

Michael Crawley (9)
The Mary Erskine & Stewart's Melville Junior School

THE FIREWORKS

Boom, they're off,
A burst of colour.
Amazed people,
Watching the shooting stars go by.

The Catherine wheels
Whizz in all directions,
Raining blues, reds and whites,
Sparklers burst like exploding stars,
Roman candles look like flickering fire.

They're melting away,
The last big cracker dies down,
Another Bonfire Night over,
Now all that's left of Bonfire Night are the ashes.

Kathryn Donnelly (9)
The Mary Erskine & Stewart's Melville Junior School

THE MOON TIDE

The night was dark upon the sky
That silver thing was floating
I could hear the sea a-lapping
Upon the rocky beach a-flapping
A big hole of silver
That laps upon the earth
The sea is cold and watery
It's icy to the feel
Oh, that noise, a wave so big
It's like a hand grabbing in the air
Against the silver moon.

Jacqueline Kahn (9)
The Mary Erskine & Stewart's Melville Junior School

FIREWORKS

In the night sky, down came sparkling showers of fire,
Fountains of different colours glittering down to Earth,
Like twisting, fiery flowers,
Rising like bombing rockets.

Rainbow-coloured domes,
Rattling and screeching all night long.
Dazzling in the night sky,
As people watch them streaming down.

Sounds like mice all the way up,
But then they all burst,
Lots of people in the town,
Until the last *bang!*

Jamie Cook (9)
The Mary Erskine & Stewart's Melville Junior School

THE FLUFF MONSTER!

There's something under the bed!
I'll check.
Agghh! It's on my knee.
Get lost Muffy!
How many times have I told you
Not to sleep under the bed?
Stupid cat!

Robbie Macdonald Colquhoun (9)
The Mary Erskine & Stewart's Melville Junior School

FIRE

Fire roars, flickers and burns,
Gobbling things up in a turn,
Fire spits like a beast
And it has a great big feast.

It always sparks,
When burning some bark,
When it flickers,
It gets stronger and thicker.

Fire rumbles, spurts and crackles,
Trapped so tight, trying to tackle
And trying to dash,
But get stuck in the ash.

Alexandra Spence (9)
The Mary Erskine & Stewart's Melville Junior School

THE TORNADO

T   is for tearing
O   is for odd
R   is for rustling
N   is for near
A   is for action
D   is for destroy
O   is for over.

Emma Bonthrone (9)
The Mary Erskine & Stewart's Melville Junior School

FIRE

Roasting in the fireplace
Roaring like a bear
Sizzling just like sausages
It will give you a big stare

Crackling in the distance
Hissing like a snake
Sparkling like a firework
On the fire you bake

Rumbling on through the woods
It sounds like a gunshot
Squirting like a water gun
Beware, the fire is hot!

Jennifer Smith (9)
The Mary Erskine & Stewart's Melville Junior School

FIRE

Roaring and raging, out of control,
Blown by strong winds,
Turning everything it passes into smouldering cinders,
Blazing and crackling, leaving the trees black and fizzing,
The undergrowth burns black as charcoal
And the sky is filled with smoke.

Calum MacDonald (10)
The Mary Erskine & Stewart's Melville Junior School

FIRE

As the fire roars like a bear
Down it gobbles everything that's in its path
It moves faster and faster
It spits and sparks

That crackling fire
It is twisting and turning the world around
It draws the trees upward
Towards the fire

Pulls them under
Pulls them away forever and ever
To destroy destiny
To carry on destroying.

Abigail Radford (9)
The Mary Erskine & Stewart's Melville Junior School

THE FLAMING FIRE

Sparks like stars
Sparkling like fireworks
Crackling like ovens
And spitting like snakes
Oh! What shall I do?
Oh! What shall I do?
Roaring like lions
Rumbling like an earthquake
Destroying everything in its path.

Corey Hastings (9)
The Mary Erskine & Stewart's Melville Junior School

FIRE

The fire is burning, crackling and spitting
The fire is moving, roaring loudly
You hear the trees falling, bursting into flames
People are crying for help

The fire is hissing, spitting, sizzling
The fire is raging, coming nearer and nearer
You hear it cracking, crashing, burning
The flames are rising higher and higher

The fire is sparkling, squirting and spitting
The fire is coming very near
It is circling and circling and circling
You look upon the ruins of people's homes.

David McArthur (9)
The Mary Erskine & Stewart's Melville Junior School

FIRE

Fire! Charging like a rhino,
Pulling trees to the ground
With a *crash!*
The fire roars like a bear in the distance,
The fire swallows everything in its path,
Leaving only cinders.
The fire still roaring and spitting like a snake
And it shifts as wind blows it on.

Neil Bowie (9)
The Mary Erskine & Stewart's Melville Junior School

FIRE!

The wind howled through burning trees, like a wolf's howl!
Bursting through the undergrowth like a hundred lions!
Sizzling like a million nettles!
Engulfing like a herd of elephants and overall
Destroying like a thousand rhinos driven mad!

Nothing can stop this fire,
It would be like trying to stop the sun set
It is a horrible thing to see
Someone running out of a burning building
Like a living torch

Howling! Bursting! Sizzling!
Engulfing! Destroying!
It's fire!

Alexander Robles-Thomé (9)
The Mary Erskine & Stewart's Melville Junior School

FIRE!

The fire was roaring, burning and sparkling,
The fire was spreading tree to tree.
The fire looked like an eagle,
It was spitting like a snake.
It was spreading out like a lake.
It blew up a rock,
This could give anyone a shock.
The fire got wider and wider,
This is like a real fire.

James Green (9)
The Mary Erskine & Stewart's Melville Junior School

THE DREAM

I had a dream once, long ago,
about castles, unicorns and fluffy, white snow.
A princess was captured in a tall, tall tower,
locked in a room by a frightening power.
Her attempts to escape were always in vain,
so she prayed for freedom to ease her pain.
In the middle of winter, a prince rode by
and saw the princess away up high.
The prince called to her from down below,
up to his thighs in cold, thick snow.
He reached for his rope and coiled it tight
and threw it to her with all his might.
She climbed down the rope and into his arms,
'Come with me, I own unicorn farms . . .'

Kirsten Mills (9)
The Mary Erskine & Stewart's Melville Junior School

HOW TO MAKE A KITTEN COSY

She needs a soft head like a tennis ball
She needs sharp, pointed whiskers
She needs white, pointed teeth
She need eyes as big as buttons
She needs a nose, as squashed as a ping-pong ball
She needs eyes that glow in the dark
She needs a warm house and a loving family.

Nompilo Chigaru (9)
The Mary Erskine & Stewart's Melville Junior School

I Love You Bahrain

I love you even though
you had little to do.
I love you even though
you burned me.
I love you even though
you didn't let me out in summer
without sunblock or a hat.
I love you even though
you only had one season.
I love you even though
you were a desert.
I love you even though
you were surrounded by sea water.
I love you very much
because you gave me birth there.
I will never forget you.

Nicholas J W Hay (9)
The Mary Erskine & Stewart's Melville Junior School

Crocodile

He lurks under the water
  His snout and eyes revealed
    His body armour and teeth concealed
      He stalks his prey slowly
        Waiting for the right moment
          His bright, sharp eyes fixed to hunt
            His toothy grin widens as he spots
              His next meal.

Matthew Saunders (9)
The Mary Erskine & Stewart's Melville Junior School

THE KITE

As I was walking down the beach,
I saw a pretty little girl raising a kite,
The way it went diving and flapping,
Swooshing, soaring.

The wind was hissing in a horrible way,
But that didn't make the girl not want to play.

The laughter on her jolly face,
The freedom like she was going to run a race.
The wonder, the joy on the little girl's face,
Even though the whistling wind was on her face.

Twirling and turning, twisting around,
As the girl's pink kite fell to the ground.

Sophie Riddle (9)
The Mary Erskine & Stewart's Melville Junior School

MY BIKE

I love you though your chain always falls off
I love you though your paint has faded
I love you though your gear changes when I start
I love you though your wheels get punctured
I love you though your brakes are rusty
I love you when I glide through the puddles
I love you though your handle is ripped
I love you when you zoom past plants
I love you though your seat shakes
I love you bike, I really do.

Connell Davidson (9)
The Mary Erskine & Stewart's Melville Junior School

THERE'S SOMETHING IN MY BED!

There's something in my bed,
It smells like it's been dead!
There's something behind my door,
It sounds like a wild boar!

There's something in my drawer,
It sounds like the third world war!
There's something in my bin,
It sounds like a stone, hitting tin!

There's something under my sheets,
I feel it licking my feet!
But when I picked up my covers,
There was my dog, with all his brothers!

Callum Pirie (9)
The Mary Erskine & Stewart's Melville Junior School

HOW TO MAKE A MONKEY

A monkey needs a tail like a bendy wire
It needs two legs like a long pencil case
It needs a head like a flat plate
It needs two eyes like buttons
It needs a wet nose like a leaf
It needs ears like two small sponges
It needs two arms like yo-yos
It needs a mouth like a letter box
It needs teeth and claws like pins
And lastly a bendy back to do tricks.

Lucy Millar (9)
The Mary Erskine & Stewart's Melville Junior School

THE KITE

I am but a kite,
Soaring through the sky across the open sea of clouds,
I dance with my partner of whom is far down below,
Laughing with joy,
I have freedom and whistle wherever I go
And give happiness to all those who wield me.
I will forever fly until weariness grows too heavy
And I fall, I fall down to the deadly jaws beneath.
I no longer shall fly, I will be left bruised and tattered,
No longer is my use.
I now rest there, ever to this day.

Ben Johnstone (9)
The Mary Erskine & Stewart's Melville Junior School

THE KITE

The kite soared into the air,
Swooping and dancing,
Twirling and twisting,
Whistling and whooshing.
The freedom of it tugging,
Hissing and swaying,
Flapping and diving,
Accelerating and slowing.
The rejoice of holding the string,
While it whistled in the air,
The wind blowing it sweetly.

Murray Tainton (9)
The Mary Erskine & Stewart's Melville Junior School

WEATHER

Weather, weather,
Why do you change?
Weather, weather,
You always rearrange.
From wind to snow,
Blowing from east to west.
Vibrant colours,
At your best.
A journey from
Shooting stars to Milky Way.
Changing into a
Colourful day.
A sunrise of ruby red,
And a sky of sapphire blue.
All of a sudden,
The cirrus cloud drifted into view.

Edward Hipwell (9)
The Mary Erskine & Stewart's Melville Junior School

THE OLD BEECH TREE

At the bottom of the garden stands an old beech
The hungry squirrels, red and brown
Collect nuts only they can reach

The tree is the home of many of our feathered friends
Sparrows, blue tits, blackbirds
The list never ends.

Beneath the tree at the base of the trunk
Creep creepy-crawlies
For them a very perfect bunk.

Jenni MacFarlane (9)
The Mary Erskine & Stewart's Melville Junior School

THE KITE

Soaring through the air as if a bird,
Whooshing round in circles,
Freedom.
Hissing like the waves of the tide,
Dancing like a human,
Rejoice.
Bounding for joy like celebrations,
Blowing in the air,
Whooshing.
Twisting and turning through the clouds,
Diving like a bird crashing into the sea,
Swaying.
Flapping like the sound of ducks,
Tugging with the wind,
Blowing.
Whistling through the air,
Falling down in the air,
Soaring.
What a beautiful day.

Charlotte Cruickshank (9)
The Mary Erskine & Stewart's Melville Junior School

THE KITE

The kite is whistling and swooping through the air,
As I stand on the hill and guide it to the fair.
It dances like a person right through the clouds
And I feel so free, a tiger out of the zoo grounds.
It glides through the sky,
As I watch it go very high.

Jenny Boyd (8)
The Mary Erskine & Stewart's Melville Junior School

THE AMAZING, SWOOPING KITE

I can swoop and dance and flutter,
Oh yes, oh yes I can!
I can dive and bounce and whistle
Wherever I am!
I can swing and twist and rejoice!
For I am, yes I am, an
Amazing, tugging bouncer!
A fantastic, soaring kite!

My owner can't control me,
He can't, he can't, he can't!
While I whoosh and skip and twirl
And neither can his aunt!
They yell at me,
Don't go too high,
It's time to come for tea
And down I have to fly,
The amazing, swooping kite!

Alice McLeish (9)
The Mary Erskine & Stewart's Melville Junior School

THE KITE

The kite twisting through the sky,
See the kite glide so high,
Watch it dance through the clouds,
I wonder why it has to come down?
As it swoops and looks so happy,
It suddenly crashes - *bang!*

Isla Chlebowska (9)
The Mary Erskine & Stewart's Melville Junior School

THE KITE

Twisting and twirling,
A kite I see.
The wind blowing,
Tugging and pulling,
That kite is swirling.

Swaying and soaring,
It's hard to control.
I just can't
Stop that kite,
That kite is tugging.

Whooshing and hissing,
It's pulling too hard.
Bouncing and flapping,
It needs freedom,
It's that wind again.

Diving and dancing,
It's flapping too hard.
Here are birds,
Wind's still blowing,
Pop! It's floating down.

Andrew Warnock (9)
The Mary Erskine & Stewart's Melville Junior School

RAIN

The rain came down like open taps.
The rain came down like flying cats.
The rain came down and just wouldn't stop.
Then the sun came out and made us hot.

Alexandra Hussey (9)
The Mary Erskine & Stewart's Melville Junior School

KITE

I own a kite which I really, really like
Because it goes twisting, turning and swooping.
One day that kite flew away
And never came back till the very next day.
But when it came back, I was greatly surprised,
Because I never thought it would come back.
This kite has my favourite colours,
Green, red and amber,
Plus some more that I really don't know –
So I just ignore them.
This kite that I like is a brilliant wee kite
That I will never part with.

Steven Runciman (9)
The Mary Erskine & Stewart's Melville Junior School

THE KITE

A soaring diamond in the sky,
Flapping and whistling in the wind.
Hissing at me to free it,
To let it dance with the stars.
Twisting and twirling in the clouds,
Leaping on all the sun's rays.
Darting and dashing above everything else,
Swooping and diving with the birds.
As it dances and twirls, swoops and curls,
I laugh and fly it higher.

Megan Girdwood (9)
The Mary Erskine & Stewart's Melville Junior School

THE KITE

Fly up, up, up,
Swoop, swoop, swoop.
Not too high,
Blow, blow, blow.
Twisting and twirling,
Up to the sky.
Fly, fly, fly,
But not too high.

Soaring away,
Dance, dance, dance.
Whooshing and swaying,
Soar up, but not too high.
Be free, free, free.

Jemma Welsh (9)
The Mary Erskine & Stewart's Melville Junior School

THE KITE

The sound of freedom,
I want to rejoice.
When I feel it tug,
Magic comes to life.

It twirls while flying,
Whooshing here and there.
Whistling, swooping,
Flapping in the breeze.

Shona Goudie (9)
The Mary Erskine & Stewart's Melville Junior School

THE KITE

I said to my gran, 'Can I get that kite?'
She said, 'Yes, we'll give it a try.'
We went to the beach to give it a flight,
Bouncing, blowing, tugging, whistling in the air.
The kite that I bought yesterday is flying in the air.
Whooshing around up and down,
I now have freedom.
The wind is making the kite swoop,
The wind is making it twist and turn,
Dancing in the air.
The kite that I bought yesterday is flying in the air.

Blake Steven (9)
The Mary Erskine & Stewart's Melville Junior School

THE KITE

Soaring fiercely into the deep blue sky,
Tugging, pulling, freedom so close,
Dancing, crashing into the waves,
The wind flapping and thrashing the kite away,
Hold the string, diving and diving, wet and soggy,
No more flying,
The rope has slipped, goodbye kite,
The blue sky empty, the wind still windy,
No more flying, no more kite.

Rachel Tait (10)
The Mary Erskine & Stewart's Melville Junior School

THE KITE

Take-off,
Fast as a tornado,
The only way to fly,
I defy gravity.

I'm lost,
Soaring independence,
It's so sweet to be free,
I defy gravity.

Earth, Mars,
The only way to die,
Bad times are behind me,
Landing - Heaven's in the sky.

Ian Samson (10)
The Mary Erskine & Stewart's Melville Junior School

THE KITE

Kites are really wonderful,
They swoop,
They soar and dance,
You've got to have wind,
The sea is roaring,
The trees are rustling,
What a day for flying a kite.

Edward Jones (9)
The Mary Erskine & Stewart's Melville Junior School

The Kite

I have a kite which is blue in colour,
It bounces and twists as the day goes on.
I can hear it whistling through the air,
Dancing, fluttering and bouncing in the summer breeze.
It dives in and out of all the lovely clouds,
I love my little kite,
For it is the only kite I have.

Emma Duncanson (9)
The Mary Erskine & Stewart's Melville Junior School

Going Away

Cold, lonely
Scared and petrified
Wondering when I will go home
Thinking about my father
When will this war cease?
I look around
I am confused
No family

Nothing to eat
Friends far away
Nobody to comfort me
Thinking about my father
My mum was upset as much as I was

Finally the war has ended
I can go home
See Mum
And Dad, if he is alive
My mum and me will comfort him until he is better.

Danielle Kelly (11)
Tollcross Primary School

FEELINGS

I feel happy when I am with my family.
I feel scared when my mum shouts.
I feel bored at the weekend.
I feel confident when I complete my maths.
I feel angry when my sister annoys me.
I feel tired in the morning.
I feel peaceful when I get home from school.
I feel nervous when I go to karate.
I feel frisky when I drink Coke.
I feel *fandabidozie*
Just being me!

Amie Igoe (10)
Tollcross Primary School

FEELINGS

I feel happy when I'm sleeping in my bed.
I feel funny when I bang my head.
I feel safe in my home.
I feel sad when Hibs lose.
I feel great when Hibs win.
I feel relaxed when I listen to music.
I feel upset when England get to the World Cup.
I feel really peaceful when I pat my dogs.
I feel superb when England lose.
I feel like going to sleep now.

John Stephens (10)
Tollcross Primary School

WORLD WAR II

Everyone listening to the wireless,
The announcement of war heard by all.
Everyone weeping,
Letters come through the post,
Gradually people start to accept it.

People are petrified,
Soon Poland is invaded
And they head for Britain too.

Hitler is bloodthirsty, he wants to take over the world.

Children are getting evacuated,
Some go to rotten homes,
Some go to terrific homes.
But mostly they miss their mums and dads,
They pray every night for the war to end
And to see their parents again.

Women have to work in industry,
They have to do men's work,
Mostly they miss their husbands and children.

Soldiers live and die in the war,
Some survive horrific injuries, scarred for life.

In shelters many people sit and sleep, waiting for war to end,
They know they are safe,
But what about their loved ones

The war ends in 1945,
There is a big celebration,
Every street and village are having parties.

People still mourning for their loved ones,
Some people's hearts are broken,
Some people are overjoyed.

Hitler has given up and it is victory for Britain.

We live and learn a little about it,
Wars in distant lands don't affect us much,
But maybe we begin to be afraid.

Louisa Fielding (11)
Tollcross Primary School

WILL THIS WAR EVER CEASE?

Devastation all around me,
Buildings destroyed, fallen over,
Piles of rubble, stench of garbage,
Frightened faces, chaos and destruction.

Fighters using all their might,
Fighting for their families and country,
Everyone is looking for harmony in the world,
Will this war ever cease?

Families leaving their homes,
Shifting to the countryside,
They don't want to get attacked,
Parents sending their children to protected places as evacuees,
They are waving to them with a joyless feeling in their hearts,
People passing away in front of our eyes,
Others surviving with a lot of luck,
Tears of sadness on everyone's faces,
We all want to avoid the war,
Will this war ever cease?

Shreyasi Das (10)
Tollcross Primary School

THE FEELING OF WAR

As we start a new day
This ghastly war continues
I thought that all the destruction,
Disaster was over
But I was wrong, very, very wrong

Every day we hear more news
Our successes and our failures
The wireless crackles
Speeches from Winston Churchill
Warning of imminent disaster

My son is away
Fighting in France
I used to hear from him all the time
But now I am distressed
He hasn't written
It seems like an eternity
They say, 'No news is good news,'
I hope they are right

Last night my next-door neighbour
Lost her daughter in the Blitz
I tried to pacify her
At the same time I worried even more
For my own beloved son

This hideous mistake of a war
Started in 1939
It is now 1945
I hope it ends soon before Armageddon arises

Today is the 29th of April
I really hope
I pray actually
That Hitler's reign of terror will end soon.

Paul Saunders (11)
Tollcross Primary School

THERE COULD BE A WORLD WAR III

I am a soldier
In a damp and deserted street
Why am I here?
I shouldn't be here
A German

Bang!
War is bad

Children are crying
People are dying
Mums are crying
Their children are fighting
They did not bring them up to be like this
But Hitler did
I don't know what is worse

Hitler or war?

If there is one thing I would love
It would be peace in our world
The EU is trying to do this
But sadly 56 years after World War II
The USA was bombed
There could be a World War III.

Joe O'Flaherty (12)
Tollcross Primary School

THE DREADFUL WAR

It was the 3rd September 1939
The war was dreadful
People fighting with all their might
Saving their countries
Some people dying
Some living

Children losing dads and mums
Children going on trains to protected places
Children going as evacuees with gas masks

Mums and dads going into shelters
People listening to the radios
The war is still on
Wives wishing for husbands to come back
Children praying for their dads to be okay

It is 1944 the war is still on
Most children hating where they are
Some being good and loving their new homes

Children thinking about all the incendiary bombs
Their friends dying or living

It is Christmas Day
Children getting odd Christmas presents
Children wanting to phone mums and dads

At last it is 1945
And the war is over
Children going back home
Mums kissing and hugging children
Some dads not back yet
Some children looking behind
Seeing their dads there
Some dads dead
Some in hospital
Some in homes

Hitler is now defeated
People having street parties
Glad the war is over

People putting buildings back together
Some people in distress
Losing husbands and dads
Soldiers coming out of hospitals
Feeling hurt and sad
Things will never be the same again.

Suzy Cairns (11)
Tollcross Primary School

IN THE WAR

Cold and dark
Windy
No one here
I have no family
To come to me
I pray all night
That the war will end
It does not stop
It goes on
Getting worse and worse
I can't stand this
All I want is my dad
To come and get me
I love him
One day he will come
And we will all be together
I can't wait.

Kathijha Zuber (11)
Tollcross Primary School

WHAT IS GREY?

Grey is when a tempest comes
And the wind is blowing strongly
Bad news as well
With everyone crying

When the rain is falling
And people are thinking deeply
I will be in my bed
Falling quietly in a grey sleep

Grey is the colour of my mother's skirt
And the colour of the sky when angry
The colour of an elephant, big and brave
And a small mouse, lovely and good

Grey is the colour of the river
That flows down the hills
Grey is the colour of the rocks
That are beside the sparkling waterfall

Grey is the colour of the baby squirrels,
Don't forget them!
And the doves that are grey, so pretty
Flying over the world

Grey is the colour of the judges, horrible and sharp
With their nasty grey wigs
But what about the small hedgehogs
Which play on top of Las Hill?

Grey is my favourite colour
And don't forget that!
Because it is so good-tempered
And strong and cross.

Miriam Clark (9)
Tollcross Primary School

WHAT WAR IS LIKE

I'm shivering in the trench
Wet, cold and scared
Screams coming from every direction
Bombs exploding all the time
The machine guns shooting constantly

I look at the sky
All I can see is smoke and blackness
All my friends are being shot
Some suffering
Some dying right away

I've been shot in the shoulder
I had to go to the medics
I was out for three weeks
Now I am back
I hate it!

I'm still shivering in a mucky trench
I'm soaked to the bone, freezing and frightened
Screams coming from every direction
Bombs exploding all the time
The machine guns shooting constantly

Will I ever get freedom?
Will I ever see my family again?
Will this war ever end?

Colin Cunningham (11)
Tollcross Primary School

THE SOLDIER

The slums were his home from when he was born
He wakes up each morning stinking and sweaty
No clothes to wear
No food to eat

He signs up for *war*
But bleeding on the battlefields
In cold, dark and muddy trenches
Bombs *explode* all around him
Squeaking tanks make him wish he was back
In the slums with his mum

His dad was in the war
But he was shot by the Nazis
Assassinated!

Then the sound of gunshots fade away
There is a sudden cry of victory!
The war is over.

James Hamilton (11)
Tollcross Primary School

WHAT IS PINK?

Pink is the colour of the elephant in your dream
Pink is the colour of a girl dancing
Pink is a pig in a pen
Pink is the colour of a mouse's nose
And so is the colour of my garden hose

Pink is the colour of the house next door
Pink is the colour of a little girl's dress
Pink is the colour of the sky when the sun goes down
Pink is the colour of my socks

Pink is the colour of my auntie's nails
Pink is the colour of painted snails
Pink is the colour of the letter in the mail
Pink is the colour of Bagpuss' tail

Pink is the colour of the scones my mum bakes
Pink is the colour of the soup my dad makes
Pink is the colour of my party cakes
Pink is the colour of the rakes.

Lilidh Macleod (9)
Tollcross Primary School

WHAT IS GREEN?

Green is grass,
Upon the hills.
Green is when you throw up
And you feel so sick.
Green is the colour of Nessy,
As she goes up and down in the loch.
Green is the seaweed
At the bottom of the sea.

Green is the colour of monsters,
With black and yellow teeth.
Green is a bit of Celtic strip,
Playing at Parkhead.
Green is the colour of fish
In big lochs.
Green is the colour of leaves,
Upon the high trees.

Green, green, green,
It's everywhere.

Catriona MacMahon (8)
Tollcross Primary School

WHAT IS BLUE?

Blue is my favourite colour and Adam's
The sky is blue and the sea and other colours
My eyes are blue and Adam's too
My pencil is blue and Colin's too

My bathroom is blue and the bath too
My mum has lots of bluebells in her garden
My shoes are blue with kangaroos
Big, blue boots to go in the puddles

My granny goes to Loch Gorm
My cousin has a big, blue boat
And a bright blue house in Islay

A big, blue whale swimming in the sea
With a nice dolphin, hee, hee, hee
A big, blue waterfall splashing in the lake
Blue is the colour of the paper I make
Blue is the colour of Lilidh's bottle.

Rachael Moncrieff (9)
Tollcross Primary School

WHAT IS RED?

Red is the colour of a ring.
Red is the colour of a car.
Red is the colour of running.
Red is the colour of a bar.

Red is the colour of a rug.
Red is the colour of the phone.
Red is the colour of a bug.
Red is the colour of a bone.

Red is the colour of a ball.
Red is the colour of a man.
Red is the colour of the wall.
Red is the colour of a van.

Red is the colour of a spanner.
Red is the colour of a vest.
Red is the colour of a banner.
Red is the best!

Alexander Macdonald (10)
Tollcross Primary School

WHAT IS YELLOW?

You get lots of things yellow,
Like pencils and pens and paint,
You get doors and stairs and
Loads of souvenirs.

Like clothes and shoes
And wood and sawdust,
There is yellow in fire,
Yellow is a colour of life.

You get balls the colour yellow,
The sun is bright yellow,
You can see yellow in the dark,
A banana has the colour of yellow.

Lightning is the colour yellow,
There are T-shirts that are yellow,
Trousers are yellow too,
Yellow is light!

Calum Macleod (10)
Tollcross Primary School

FEELINGS

I feel happy when I am playing with my friends.
I feel annoyed when my little brother does not get out of my room.
I feel frisky when I have wine.
I feel nervous when I am about to get a test.
I feel sad when I think about my granddad.
I feel impatient when I need to go to the loo and someone else
is using it.
I feel peaceful when I am sitting playing dominoes at my
granny's house.
I feel frightened when my dog makes noises when I'm in bed.
I feel moany when I have to do the dishes.
I feel stressed when I have a hard day at school.

Amy Purnell (10)
Tollcross Primary School

FEELINGS

I feel happy when I am with my friends.
I feel tired in the morning.
I feel scared in the dark.
I feel annoyed when my sister goes on my bed.
I feel *impatient* when my mum is in the bath and I need the toilet.
I feel famished when I come in from school.
I feel nervous when I'm on stage.
I feel excited on Christmas Eve.
I feel confused when two people talk to me at the same time.
I fee peaceful when I go to bed.

Rosie Paterson (10)
Tollcross Primary School

FLIP-FLOP

Hip hop, hip hop
I've lost a flip-flop
I've looked high and I've looked low
I've looked everywhere that I go
'Silly billy,' said my mum
I'm off to play my drum
I've still not found that one flip-flop
So tomorrow I'm going to the shop
Hip hop, hip hop
I've still not found that old flip-flop
Hip hop, hip hop
Off you trot.

Ellen McGhee (10)
Tollcross Primary School

WHAT IS GREEN?

Upon the mountains the grass is green
Under the sea the fish are green
The Loch Ness monster is green
You are green when you are sick
Lots of cars are green
The colour green is in the Celtic strip
I've got green shorts
The sea is green
I've got a green watch
I've got green shoes
Green is the best colour.

Connor Johnson (8)
Tollcross Primary School

WHAT IS BLUE?

Blue is the sky on a bright summer's day
You're blue when you're feeling sad or lonely
Blue is the big, wavy sea
Coming up on the beach

Blue is when you're shivering with the cold
School jumpers, big, blue boats
Little singing bluebirds and whales in the sea
Blue all around us, blue everywhere

Blue, blue, blue and more blue!

Hannah Macleod (8)
Tollcross Primary School

WHAT IS PURPLE?

Purple is a stormy night
Purple is a day of sadness
Purple is a rocky mountain
Purple is a tiny light
Purple is a stony graveyard
Purple is a strong, hot drink
It's a warm place after the draft
It's a deep, deep smell and a poor old man
It's boiling water and church bells ringing
But purple is a massive big colour.

Euan MacLeod (9)
Tollcross Primary School

SUMMER

On the beach eating candy
When it is very sandy
Swimming along in the sea
When it is really time for tea
Going home in the car
Hoping you're not going far
Drinking juice in the garden
Burping loudly, beg your pardon
Indoors eating tea
Sweaty cat on my knee
Summer is the hottest season
I don't really know the reason.

Alice Black (10)
Trinity Primary School

WINTER

Winds blow and snow falls
Now snowflakes begin to show
Lakes frost over
Now things get lost beneath the snow
Rivers can't flow for the ice has slowly
Frosted over them

Winds blow and snow falls
Now drips of snowflakes begin to fall
And splatter off the ground.

Calum Nicholson (10)
Trinity Primary School

SUMMER

Summer is playing in the sun
Summer is having lots of fun

Summer is lying on a beach
And teachers do not have to teach

Summer is smelling the flowers
Summer is building sand towers

Summer is catching the sunrays
Summer is going on holidays

Summer is when you can fly your kites
Summer's the time to have water fights

In summer you can get a tan
And if you're hot you wave a fan

On the beach you can make sandcastles
There's no school so we have no hassles

Long lie-ins every day
Before you rush out to play

No floods, so you don't need a plumber
Everyone loves a nice warm summer.

Nikki Wilson (10)
Trinity Primary School

AUTUMN

Autumn leaves on the ground,
Swirling round, round and round,
The cold wind blows them away,
But they will come back another day.

Autumn days can be cold,
Autumn is very old,
Autumn clothes are very warm,
They will keep you cosy if there is a storm.

Alexandra Warren (10)
Trinity Primary School

HOLIDAYS

Pack your bags, it's time to leave
The suitcase is heavy, give it a heave
Holidays

You're up in the air
Your hair is everywhere
Holidays

We are finally here at the hotel
So many stairs to climb, I nearly fell
Holidays

It's the next day, it's time to play
We are going off to the bay
Holidays

The week has passed – so fast
I wish it would last longer
Holidays.

Danielle Cook (10)
Trinity Primary School

SUMMERTIME

It's summertime again, yippee!
Who wants to come to the beach with me?
I'll put away my woolly hat,
Today I'm not going to need that.

We're going away in our caravan
And we'll have a barbecue every night if we can.
I'm going down to see the sea
And maybe get a lolly to have after tea.

I'm so glad I'm not at school,
I wonder what's in this rock pool?
Maybe I should get back,
The sky is turning a little bit black.

After tea, I go to bed,
Happy as I can be.
Here I lie,
Looking up at the starry summer sky.

I want summer to never pass by!

Rachel Pont (10)
Trinity Primary School

SUMMER

Summer, summer, red-hot days
Summer, summer, lovely days
Summer, summer, scent days
Summer, summer, busy bee days.

Matthew Renshaw (9)
Trinity Primary School

AUTUMN

Autumn days have come
time to jump in the pile of leaves
climb the naked trees

All the fun things to do
go in the countryside
and hear the cows *moo!*
As the leaves crumble
they fall in a big tumble

But the best thing about the leaves
the colours
red, brown, yellow and maroon.

Christopher Murray (10)
Trinity Primary School

AUTUMN

It's a cold, windy day
No one will come out to play
It's autumn
Leaves swooshing down to the ground
But there is no sound
It's autumn
When I walk over the leaves
They crackle and crunch
When will it be time for lunch?

Danielle Willis (10)
Trinity Primary School

AUTUMN DAYS

I run through the woods
I stand on all the leaves
I hear the leaves crunching
Autumn days

I run back home
I see the bare trees
All around on the ground, orange leaves
Autumn days

I go inside, it's really dark
I feel the fire
I go near, I see it spark
Autumn days

I run back outside
I make a big hill made out of leaves
I jump in the leaves, I hear the crackling
Autumn days

I see the leaves twirl, twist
I look up at the sky, it's dull
I have to go inside.

Lauren Stoddart (10)
Trinity Primary School

AUTUMN

Autumn is back, cold and windy,
Leaves twisting, twirling into bundles.
Children running, jumping, kicking leaves about,
Drifting around the playground and lying.

Children have their hats and scarves on,
That's when I know autumn's back.
Window creak, doors open and shut,
Umbrellas turn inside out, hats blow away.

Danielle Clark (10)
Trinity Primary School

WINTER

Pitter-patter on the roof
Snowflakes blow around the sky
Gentle sleet flies swiftly down
Pitter-patter on the roof
A storm comes and snow

In the garden you will go
With freezing ice and rain

Battling down the hailstones go
Pitter-patter on the roof
Footprints grow across the yard
Freezing feet in soggy wellies

Hats and gloves, a purple scarf
Drip drop goes the ice sticks
That drop onto the ground
I'm home at last and no more snow.

Hannah Baillie (10)
Trinity Primary School

WINTER

To wake up to the wind blowing in,
To put the warm soup tin in the bin,
To stagger out into the frost,
To try and find the scarf you've lost.
To take your dog out for a walk,
To fall upon the slippery rock,
To watch the lightning strike,
To put away your summery bike.
To have a sore throat and cough and sneeze,
To look at your red, frozen knees,
To swallow that medicine,
To see the sky so grim.
To finally go to bed,
To dream about the freezing shed,
There is one thing I have to say,
It must be winter every day.

Rachel Edwards (9)
Trinity Primary School

SUMMERTIME

Yey, it's summer
Time for ice cream
Barbecue in the garden
The best summer there's ever been

Flowers looking pretty
Butterflies going flirty, flirty
Sunglasses for the beach
And the bee makes people screech!

Soon it will be the holidays
Time for going outdoors
It'll be really nice and warm
And there definitely won't be any storms

Now after all that fun
I'm ready to go to bed
No need for hot water bottles
For it's summertime again.

Naomi Todd (10)
Trinity Primary School

SUMMER

I wake up to the sunshine
Beating through my window

Flowers looking pretty
Bees flying over the flowers
Butterflies drinking nectar

The golden, sandy beach
Shells muddled all over the golden sand
The sea rushing up then back again

Ice cream dripping to the ground
Strawberry, mint, chocolate chip, vanilla, chocolate mint!
I can't choose what flavour to have!

I watch the children building sandcastles
Making moats leading from the sea

I wake up to the sunshine
Beating through my window.

Louise Taylor (10)
Trinity Primary School

WINTER

The cold wind blows,
Ice sticks to my toes,
The days seem dark,
The dogs don't bark,
Winter is the best time of the year!

Hot cups of coffee waiting for me,
Presents sitting under the Christmas tree,
The fire crackling, burning high,
Smoke floating up the chimney to the sky,
Winter is the best time of the year!

Now it's up to bed, I blow my nose,
A hot water bottle to warm my toes,
I say goodnight to the winter's day
And fall asleep while my kittens play,
Winter is the best time of the year!

Jamie Woods (10)
Trinity Primary School

SUMMER

Hot and sweaty
Rolling in the sand
Looking like a sand monster

Ice cream melting
Going up your nose
Going in the outdoor swimming pool

Burgers sizzling
You sizzling.

Carri-Ann Campbell (9)
Trinity Primary School

AUTUMN'S WAYS

I like to see how autumn can start,
Bright blooms turn golden brown, it's a work of art.

Kicking leaves that make a crackling sound,
Making a three foot tall mound.

Fireside's sparks fly after their rest,
For summer has gone and they're back to their best.

All leaves swooping high and low,
Just letting them fall like so.

Autumn is the best chance to play, before it's too cold,
Swirling around in a great colour of gold.

Hazel Lauren Dubourdieu (10)
Trinity Primary School

AUTUMN

It's
Autumn
It's very cold
Time to keep warm
Stay in your house
Stay by the nice warm fire
It's autumn again, go outside
And play in the leaves
You'll hear crunch
Crackle, crackle
Scruff, scruff
Scruff.

Derek Banks (10)
Trinity Primary School

I'M A LITTLE MOUSE

Winter's near
Winter's here
Be careful you don't slip!

Frost on your fingertips
Wiggle your hips
So it will fall onto the cold, thick snow

The river
Hardly ever
Flows anymore

So walk and open the door
Into a warm, cosy house
I need warmth
Because I'm a little mouse!

Sarah Gegan (10)
Trinity Primary School